HSK 2 GRAMMAR WORKBOOK

CHINESE SENTENCE STRUCTURE

BY LEONG

Copyright © 2020 B.Y Leong

ISBN: 9798682370382

All rights reserved. This book or parts thereof may not be reproduced in any form, stored in any retrieval system, or transmitted in any form by any means—electronic, mechanical, photocopy, recording, or otherwise— without prior written permission of the publisher, except as provided by applicable law.

Any references to historical events, real people, or real places are used fictitiously. Other names, characters, places and events are products of the author's imagination, and any resemblances to actual events or places or persons, living or dead, is entirely coincidental.

Publisher: Leong Bik Yoke

C1013 Centum@Oasis Corporate Park,

No.2, Jalan PJU1A/2,

Ara Damansara

47301 Petaling Jaya,

Selangor MALAYSIA

feedback@allmusing.net

Table of Contents

INTRODUCTION 7

SENTENCE STRUCTURE EXERCISES 9

ANSWER 136

HSK Book Series: -

HSK 1 Grammar Workbook – Chinese Sentence Structure

HSK 2 Grammar Workbook – Chinese Sentence Structure

HSK 3 Grammar Workbook – Chinese Sentence Structure

HSK 1 Storybook

HSK 1 Storybook Vol 2

HSK 1 Storybook Vol 3

HSK 2 Storybook Vol 1

HSK 2 Storybook Vol 2

HSK 2 Storybook Vol 3

HSK 3 Storybook Vol 1

HSK 3 Storybook Vol 2

HSK 3 Storybook Vol 3

HSK 4 Storybook Vol 1

HSK 4 Storybook Vol 2

HSK 4 Storybook Vol 3

HSK 1,2,3,4 Flashcards with Audio and Writing Practice Sheet

HSK 1 Vocabulary Writing Practice Sheet

HSK 2 Vocabulary Writing Practice Sheet

HSK 3 Vocabulary Writing Practice Sheet

HSK 4 Vocabulary Writing Practice Sheet

HSK 5 Vocabulary Writing Practice Sheet

HSK 6 Vocabulary Writing Practice Sheet

and other titles coming soon.

Subscribe to our newsletter to be informed of new titles.

Go to www.allmusing.net to download sample chapters and free audio files.

INTRODUCTION

This book consists of over 1100 sentences, written with only HSK 2 Vocabulary words. Purpose of this book is to get you familiarise with the Chinese sentence structure/word order.

Due to the limit in vocabulary, some of the sentences are partial sentences. The hints to complete the question are provided as reference, you may cover it up once you are more familiar.

Why Do you Need to Learn Sentence Structure?

Even as a beginner, you should start to learn about the Chinese sentence structure. Using sentences as your base gives you the benefit of learning how to speak straight away. You will also be learning about how tones are put together in the sentence and how words interact within sentences.

Chinese language has very complicated grammar rules. There are general grammar rules followed by a long list of exceptions. Further, Chinese is a very precise language. Even when you use the same words, but in a different order, it could give a completely different meaning.

HSK 2 Grammar Workbook will help you practise forming proper Chinese sentences with vocabulary that you are already familiar with. Even if you get a lot of sentence structure wrong in the beginning, but as you go along, you will learn from your mistakes and get better. This is definitely more fun than purely memorising the grammar rules.

The basic formation of a Chinese Sentence

1. Subject + Verb (你去)
2. Subject + Verb + Object (你去学校)
3. Subject + Time + Verb + Object （你今天去学校）or Time + Subject + Verb + Object (今天我去学校)

4. Subject + Verb + Object + 吗 (converts the sentence to a question) (你今天去学校吗?)

5. In a simple positive descriptive statement, a degree adverb or a complement of degree should be used. Subject + Degree + Adjective (你很漂亮).

These few simple rules should get you started in forming proper Chinese sentences.

We find reading will also help in your learning progress. You should check out the **HSK Storybook series**, which are also written with the respective HSK level words. Please go to www.allmusing.net to download sample chapters and audio files.

There is an online version of these exercises available at www.allmusing.net/hsktest/

Enjoy!

B. Y Leong

SENTENCE STRUCTURE EXERCISES

1. I don't know what to wear.
   A: 不   B: 我   C: 好   D: 什么   E: 穿   F: 知道

2. I'm eating noodles.
   A: 在   B: 吃   C: 面条   D: 我

3. I didn't bring a cell phone.
   A: 我   B: 带   C: 没有   D: 手机

4. What are you laughing at?
   A: 什么   B: 你   C: 笑   D: 在

5. When will we arrive tomorrow?
   A: 我们   B: 什么   C: 时候   D: 到   E: 明天

6. How far is your school?
   A: 学校   B: 有   C: 远   D: 你   E: 多   F: 的

7. I don't know yet.
   A: 我   B: 不   C: 知道   D: 还

8. Please tell me something.
   A: 请   B: 一些   C: 我   D: 告诉   E: 事情

9. You can start now.
   A: 了　B: 可以　C: 开始　D: 你　E: 现在

10. How do you know it's my favorite?
    A: 的　B: 喜欢　C: 我　D: 知道　E: 最　F: 是　G: 怎么　H: 你　I: 那

11. She wasn't there when I called her.
    A: 打电话　B: 我　C: 在　D: 她　E: 她　F: 给　G: 的　H: 时候　I: 不

12. Please give me some water.
    A: 我　B: 点　C: 水　D: 给　E: 请

13. Do you have anything to do today?
    A: 什么　B: 你　C: 有　D: 今天　E: 做　F: 要　G: 事情　H: 吗

14. Where were you yesterday?
    A: 在　B: 您　C: 哪儿　D: 昨天

15. Why are you here?
    A: 你　B: 为什么　C: 在　D: 这

16. I want you to go.
    A: 希望　B: 去　C: 我　D: 你

17. Could you tell me how to get to the railway station, please?
    A: 怎么　B: 火车站　C: 请问　D: 走　E: 去

18. She has no real friends.
    A: 她 B: 朋友 C: 没有 D: 真正 E: 的

19. She didn't tell me her name.
    A: 的 B: 名字 C: 她 D: 她 E: 我 F: 没有 G: 告诉

20. It is our job to help her.
    A: 是 B: 帮助 C: 她 D: 我们 E: 的 F: 工作

21. Is that what you want?
    A: 的 B: 要 C: 是 D: 吗 E: 这 F: 你

22. You're talking too much.
    A: 多 B: 说 C: 得 D: 太 E: 了 F: 你

23. He likes singing and dancing.
    A: 他 B: 喜欢 C: 也 D: 跳舞 E: 唱歌 F: 喜欢

24. She is my sister.
    A: 的 B: 姐姐 C: 我 D: 是 E: 她

25. There is tea tea and coffee, what do you like?
    A: 茶 B: 和 C: 喜欢 D: 有 E: 你 F: 什么 G: 咖啡

26. I want us to do it together.
    A: 我 B: 要 C: 一起 D: 我们 E: 做

27. He likes traveling very much.
    A: 喜欢   B: 他   C: 很   D: 旅游

28. I'm waiting for the bus.
    A: 公共汽车   B: 我   C: 等   D: 在

29. I like dancing, too.
    A: 也   B: 我   C: 跳舞   D: 喜欢

30. It is eating rice.
    A: 正在   B: 吃   C: 米饭   D: 它

31. She's going to bed.
    A: 了   B: 睡觉   C: 要   D: 她

32. Do you know who she is?
    A: 谁   B: 她   C: 是   D: 知道   E: 吗   F: 你

33. Will she come, too?
    A: 吗   B: 来   C: 会   D: 她   E: 也

34. Do you have a pencil?
    A: 有   B: 吗   C: 铅笔   D: 您

35. I'm prettier than you.
    A: 比   B: 漂亮   C: 你   D: 我

HSK 2 GRAMMAR WORKBOOK

36. She likes dancing very much.
    A: 喜欢 B: 她 C: 跳舞 D: 很

37. Let's take a taxi.
    A: 出租车 B: 去 C: 我们 D: 坐 E: 吧

38. Because everyone has no money.
    A: 了 B: 钱 C: 大家 D: 因为 E: 没有 F: 都

39. I'd like to have noodles.
    A: 面条 B: 我 C: 想 D: 吃

40. It was cold this morning.
    A: 冷 B: 今天 C: 早上 D: 很

41. I don't like cats and my brother doesn't like them either.
    A: 弟弟 B: 猫 C: 不 D: 也 E: 不 F: 我 G: 喜欢 H: 喜欢 I: 我

42. You mustn't come with us.
    A: 不 B: 我们 C: 一起 D: 去 E: 和 F: 你 G: 可以

43. Because it's too big.
    A: 了 B: 太 C: 大 D: 因为 E: 它

44. I want to go with you but I don't have time.
    A: 但是 B: 你 C: 时间 D: 我 E: 没有 F: 一起 G: 我 H: 想 I: 和 J: 去

CHINESE SENTENCE STRUCTURE

45. I know everything.
    A: 什么   B: 知道   C: 都   D: 我

46. She loves her children.
    A: 的   B: 爱   C: 她   D: 她   E: 孩子

47. I love her very much but she doesn't love me.
    A: 我   B: 她   C: 我   D: 爱   E: 不   F: 爱   G: 她   H: 但是   I: 很

48. Would you like some more tea?
    A: 来   B: 吗   C: 茶   D: 再   E: 点   F: 好

49. I know something.
    A: 我   B: 事情   C: 一些   D: 知道

50. What's wrong with your computer?
    A: 有   B: 你   C: 什么   D: 问题   E: 的   F: 电脑

51. I don't know what you mean.
    A: 你   B: 明白   C: 我   D: 不   E: 意思   F: 的

52. Do you want to know what I see?
    A: 我   B: 想   C: 看见   D: 了   E: 你   F: 什么   G: 知道   H: 吗

53. I know she doesn't love him.
    A: 爱   B: 她   C: 知道   D: 不   E: 我   F: 他

HSK 2 GRAMMAR WORKBOOK

54. He's going to bed.
    A: 了   B: 要   C: 睡觉   D: 他

55. I know she doesn't love it.
    A: 我   B: 知道   C: 爱   D: 它   E: 不   F: 她

56. There is a good chance that it will rain again.
    A: 再次   B: 下雨   C: 有   D: 可能   E: 很

57. This is your color.
    A: 的   B: 颜色   C: 这   D: 你   E: 是

58. He wants to go to the cinema with us.
    A: 我们   B: 他   C: 去   D: 想   E: 和   F: 电影   G: 一起   H: 看

59. I think you like her.
    A: 觉得   B: 喜欢   C: 她   D: 你   E: 我

60. I ate fish yesterday.
    A: 了   B: 鱼   C: 吃   D: 昨天

61. Let's go.
    A: 吧   B: 走   C: 可以   D: 了

62. I don't know what you mean.
    A: 知道   B: 不   C: 什么   D: 意思   E: 我   F: 你

63. He is taller than his brother.
    A: 比   B: 他   C: 他   D: 的   E: 高   F: 弟弟

64. I don't know when he will come again.
    A: 他   B: 来   C: 不   D: 知道   E: 再   F: 什么   G: 我   H: 时候

65. Is the student who is playing football your classmate?
    A: 踢足球   B: 的   C: 学生   D: 的   E: 你   F: 同学   G: 是   H: 吗   I: 那个   J: 正在

66. How many times have you seen this?
    A: 多少   B: 次   C: 你   D: 看过   E: 了

67. You sing for me.
    A: 你   B: 给   C: 我   D: 唱歌

68. How many watermelons are there.
    A: 西瓜   B: 多少   C: 有   D: 个

69. Do you like running?
    A: 喜欢   B: 跑步   C: 吗   D: 你

70. He likes me and I like him.
    A: 他   B: 也   C: 我   D: 喜欢   E: 喜欢   F: 他   G: 我

71. Fruit is very good for the body.
    A: 好   B: 对   C: 非常   D: 水果   E: 身体

72. I'm going for a run in the morning.
    A: 我   B: 要   C: 去   D: 早上   E: 跑步

73. Whenever he wants to get up, he will get up.
    A: 起床   B: 时候   C: 想   D: 他   E: 什么   F: 什么   G: 起床   H: 时候
    I: 就

74. Would you please leave the door open?
    A: 好   B: 吗   C: 你   D: 开   E: 把门   F: 着   G: 请

75. She helped him.
    A: 他   B: 了   C: 帮助   D: 她

76. You know who am I?
    A: 你   B: 知道   C: 我   D: 谁   E: 是

77. What's your husband's name?
    A: 什么   B: 你   C: 丈夫   D: 叫   E: 名字

78. Are you looking for a job?
    A: 在   B: 吗   C: 你   D: 工作   E: 找

79. How far is it to the airport?
    A: 机场   B: 远   C: 有   D: 到   E: 多

80. It's hot this morning.
    A: 呢   B: 很   C: 今天   D: 热   E: 早上

81. What's new?
    A: 东西   B: 有   C: 什么   D: 新

82. He goes to work by bus.
    A: 公共汽车   B: 他   C: 上班   D: 坐

83. Can I have something to eat?
    A: 可以   B: 吗   C: 我   D: 点   E: 吃   F: 东西

84. What's your favorite fruit?
    A: 什么   B: 喜欢   C: 最   D: 水果   E: 你

85. Can you give me some more tea?
    A: 能   B: 点   C: 你   D: 我   E: 给   F: 茶   G: 再   H: 吗

86. Call me tomorrow.
    A: 我   B: 明天   C: 打电话   D: 给

87. Who were you talking to?
    A: 在   B: 谁   C: 你   D: 和   E: 说话

88. I'll call you at home.
    A: 打电话   B: 家   C: 给   D: 到   E: 我   F: 你

89. You drank too much coffee.
    A: 得   B: 咖啡   C: 多   D: 太   E: 了   F: 喝   G: 你

90. Don't talk, listen to me.
    A: 听   B: 说话   C: 说   D: 别   E: 我

91. Could you open the door, please?
    A: 能   B: 吗   C: 打开   D: 把门   E: 你

92. Why didn't you go?
    A: 去   B: 不   C: 你   D: 为什么

93. Did you call me in the evening?
    A: 我   B: 了   C: 给   D: 你   E: 晚上   F: 打电话   G: 吗

94. What color is your dress?
    A: 衣服   B: 什么   C: 的   D: 你   E: 是   F: 的   G: 颜色

95. He asked my mother.
    A: 的   B: 我   C: 妈妈   D: 问   E: 他   F: 了

96. I know what you mean.
    A: 明白   B: 意思   C: 的   D: 你   E: 我

97. Do you want to play basketball now?
    A: 想   B: 打篮球   C: 吗   D: 你   E: 现在

98. He is my brother.
    A: 的   B: 他   C: 哥哥   D: 是   E: 我

99. Go in front of me.
   A: 去   B: 我   C: 前面   D: 到

100. I'll get you ready.
   A: 好   B: 的   C: 我会   D: 准备   E: 你   F: 帮

101. Does he know who I am?
   A: 他   B: 知道   C: 我   D: 谁   E: 是   F: 吗

102. Yesterday was my birthday.
   A: 生日   B: 我   C: 昨天   D: 的   E: 是

103. I don't know when he will come.
   A: 来   B: 我   C: 时候   D: 不   E: 知道   F: 他   G: 什么

104. He is my brother.
   A: 他   B: 我   C: 弟弟   D: 是

105. How old is your child?
   A: 孩子   B: 多   C: 的   D: 你   E: 了   F: 大

106. I see what you mean.
   A: 的   B: 懂   C: 我   D: 你   E: 那   F: 了   G: 意思

107. What did you eat in the morning?
   A: 了   B: 吃   C: 什么   D: 你   E: 早上

108. How much do you want?
   A: 钱   B: 要   C: 多少   D: 您

HSK 2 GRAMMAR WORKBOOK

109. I will go to see the movies.

   A: 看   B: 我   C: 电影   D: 要   E: 去

110. Do you like your new job?

   A: 的   B: 新   C: 你   D: 工作   E: 吗   F: 喜欢   G: 你

111. Why do you want to know what I'm thinking?

   A: 什么   B: 我   C: 为什么   D: 想   E: 知道   F: 想   G: 你   H: 在

112. I want to know your sister.

   A: 我   B: 想   C: 你   D: 认识   E: 姐姐

113. Would you like to dance together?

   A: 你   B: 吗   C: 一起   D: 愿意   E: 跳舞

114. When will this be ready?

   A: 时候   B: 准备   C: 好   D: 什么   E: 这个

115. Put on some clothes.

   A: 衣服   B: 上   C: 点   D: 穿

116. I'd like something delicious.

   A: 吃   B: 好吃   C: 想   D: 我   E: 的   F: 点

117. Can I have a look at your ticket?

   A: 我   B: 吗   C: 一下   D: 看   E: 您   F: 的   G: 票   H: 能

118. It's farther to our school than to the railway station.
　　A: 我们　B: 要　C: 比　D: 学校　E: 火车站　F: 去　G: 远　H: 去

119. Can you swim?
　　A: 游泳　B: 你　C: 吗　D: 能

120. Yes, I am a student, too.
　　A: 是　B: 的　C: 学生　D: 是　E: 也　F: 我

121. Let's go swimming.
　　A: 去　B: 游泳　C: 吧　D: 我们

122. Do you know his brother?
　　A: 认识　B: 吗　C: 你　D: 哥哥　E: 他

123. I think it's up to you.
　　A: 要　B: 觉得　C: 的　D: 看　E: 吧　F: 我　G: 这

124. How did you get there?
　　A: 那儿　B: 你　C: 到　D: 的　E: 怎么

125. He felt I loved her.
　　A: 我　B: 觉得　C: 她　D: 爱　E: 他

126. When do you go to work?
　　A: 什么　B: 时候　C: 你　D: 上班

127. He starts work today.
　　A: 开始　B: 今天　C: 他　D: 工作

128. I don't like playing football.
　　A: 我　B: 喜欢　C: 踢足球　D: 不

129. I wish I could go.
　　A: 可以　B: 我　C: 去　D: 希望　E: 我

130. He didn't know what he was talking about.
　　A: 他　B: 什么　C: 他　D: 说　E: 在　F: 不　G: 知道

131. Dad bought me a book.
　　A: 给　B: 爸爸　C: 我　D: 了　E: 买　F: 本书

132. Tired as I am, I have done what I can.
　　A: 已经　B: 做　C: 很　D: 能　E: 做　F: 了　G: 了　H: 我　I: 我　J: 的
　　K: 但是　L: 累　M: 我　N: 虽然

133. What do you want to say to me?
　　A: 我　B: 你　C: 什么　D: 想　E: 对　F: 说

134. I want to know who's here.
　　A: 谁　B: 知道　C: 了　D: 想　E: 来　F: 我

135. Who told you that.
　　A: 你　B: 告诉　C: 谁　D: 的

136. Don't tell him.
    A: 就   B: 告诉   C: 别   D: 他

137. No one told me where to find you.
    A: 在   B: 告诉   C: 找到   D: 我   E: 人   F: 没   G: 哪里   H: 你   I: 可以

138. What does that mean.
    A: 是   B: 什么   C: 意思   D: 这

139. I was wrong from the beginning.
    A: 一   B: 就   C: 错   D: 从   E: 我   F: 开始   G: 了

140. You can do anything.
    A: 怎么   B: 可以   C: 你   D: 都   E: 做

141. His wife is my daughter.
    A: 他   B: 女儿   C: 妻子   D: 是   E: 我

142. Call me when you have arrived.
    A: 打电话   B: 了   C: 到   D: 我   E: 给

143. I'll go and wash it.
    A: 我   B: 一   C: 去   D: 洗   E: 洗

144. What I meant is...
    A: 的   B: 意思   C: 我   D: 是

145. Does he know you love him?
    A: 他   B: 他   C: 你   D: 知道   E: 爱   F: 吗

146. We don't have much time.
    A: 的   B: 时间   C: 多   D: 不   E: 我们

147. Okay, I'll have some more.
    A: 点   B: 的   C: 我   D: 再   E: 好   F: 吃

148. I haven't read the newspaper today.
    A: 我   B: 的   C: 报纸   D: 今天   E: 没有   F: 看   G: 还

149. What are you going to do today?
    A: 什么   B: 做   C: 要   D: 今天   E: 你

150. No one knows.
    A: 也   B: 谁   C: 知道   D: 不

151. Is this the railway station?
    A: 吗   B: 这   C: 火车站   D: 是

152. Everyone is waiting for you.
    A: 都   B: 等   C: 你   D: 在   E: 大家

153. Where is your home?
    A: 的   B: 家   C: 哪   D: 在   E: 您

154. I don't understand what you mean.
   A: 我   B: 懂   C: 意思   D: 的   E: 不   F: 你

155. What's your name?
   A: 您   B: 叫   C: 什么   D: 名字

156. I'm not ready.
   A: 没   B: 还   C: 好   D: 我   E: 准备

157. Tell me what you want.
   A: 我   B: 什么   C: 要   D: 你   E: 告诉

158. He said it was likely to rain.
   A: 他   B: 可能   C: 说   D: 要   E: 下雨

159. What dishes are you doing?
   A: 做   B: 什么   C: 您   D: 在   E: 菜

160. I know her sister.
   A: 认识   B: 姐姐   C: 的   D: 我   E: 她

161. Are you busy now?
   A: 忙   B: 你   C: 现在   D: 吗

162. I don't know what you're talking about.
   A: 我   B: 在   C: 说   D: 什么   E: 知道   F: 不   G: 你

163. Do you want to travel?
A: 旅游   B: 想   C: 吗   D: 你   E: 去

164. I'm very busy right now.
A: 我   B: 现在   C: 非常   D: 忙

165. She may be in the classroom.
A: 可能   B: 在   C: 教室   D: 她   E: 里

166. Is your father busy?
A: 吗   B: 很   C: 忙   D: 你   E: 爸爸

167. Come if you can.
A: 你   B: 来   C: 来   D: 能   E: 就

168. She asked him a question.
A: 了   B: 一个   C: 她   D: 他   E: 问   F: 问题

169. You'd better have something to eat.
A: 你   B: 点   C: 最   D: 东西   E: 好吃

170. You know too much.
A: 知道   B: 你   C: 的   D: 多   E: 太   F: 了

171. Do you think there will be any problems?
A: 问题   B: 什么   C: 你   D: 有   E: 觉得   F: 会   G: 吗

172. He is busy with his work.
   A: 工作   B: 忙   C: 着   D: 他

173. I think I drank too much.
   A: 了   B: 我   C: 我   D: 喝   E: 得   F: 想   G: 多   H: 太

174. I'm learning Chinese.
   A: 正在   B: 学习   C: 我   D: 汉语

175. Are you looking for anything?
   A: 在   B: 吗   C: 什么   D: 您   E: 找

176. Has it arrived?
   A: 已经   B: 了   C: 到   D: 吗

177. He is very nice to me.
   A: 他   B: 对   C: 很   D: 好   E: 我

178. I'm not busy today.
   A: 忙   B: 今天   C: 不   D: 我

179. I don't know his last name.
   A: 的   B: 姓   C: 我   D: 他   E: 知道   F: 不

180. I said it might rain.
   A: 下雨   B: 了   C: 可能   D: 我   E: 说   F: 要

HSK 2 GRAMMAR WORKBOOK   29

181. Would you like some noodles?
    A: 来 B: 吗 C: 你 D: 面条 E: 点

182. I'd like to buy a cheaper one.
    A: 便宜 B: 我 C: 想 D: 一个 E: 的 F: 一点 G: 买

183. I can wait for you.
    A: 你 B: 等 C: 我 D: 可以

184. I'll come when I have time.
    A: 有 B: 时间 C: 来 D: 我 E: 就

185. Go wherever you like.
    A: 哪儿 B: 好 C: 就 D: 去 E: 觉得 F: 你 G: 哪儿

186. I think I'm going to bed.
    A: 要 B: 我 C: 睡觉 D: 想 E: 了 F: 去 G: 我

187. Are you in good health?
    A: 你 B: 好 C: 身体 D: 吗

188. She likes singing very much.
    A: 她 B: 唱歌 C: 喜欢 D: 非常

189. Please tell me your name.
    A: 的 B: 名字 C: 你 D: 我 E: 告诉 F: 请

190. Her sister is older than my brother.
    A: 姐姐   B: 比   C: 哥哥   D: 大   E: 我   F: 她

191. What are you laughing at?
    A: 你   B: 什么   C: 笑   D: 呢

192. Do you want to go swimming?
    A: 游泳   B: 去   C: 想   D: 你   E: 吗

193. Don't come into my room.
    A: 进   B: 别   C: 我   D: 房间   E: 的

194. I know you don't like him.
    A: 知道   B: 我   C: 不   D: 他   E: 你   F: 喜欢

195. It may rain tomorrow.
    A: 下雨   B: 会   C: 明天   D: 可能

196. She may be taller than you.
    A: 比   B: 高   C: 她   D: 可能   E: 你

197. Why don't you sleep?
    A: 怎么   B: 你   C: 不   D: 还   E: 睡觉

198. Let's start eating.
    A: 吃   B: 吧   C: 我们   D: 开始

199. No one knows why.

   A: 谁   B: 知道   C: 也   D: 为什么   E: 不

200. How far is it to the railway station?

   A: 火车站   B: 远   C: 多   D: 有   E: 到

201. I'm going to see him today.

   A: 今天   B: 要   C: 去   D: 他   E: 我   F: 看

202. I got to know him last year.

   A: 认识   B: 他   C: 了   D: 我   E: 去年

203. I'm sorry I was wrong.

   A: 了   B: 我   C: 对不起   D: 错

204. She also likes to eat noodles.

   A: 喜欢   B: 她   C: 吃   D: 面条   E: 也

205. I'm so glad you came.

   A: 你   B: 很   C: 高兴   D: 了   E: 我   F: 来

206. Is it still raining?

   A: 还   B: 在   C: 下雨   D: 吗

207. She is a very good teacher.

   A: 非常   B: 她   C: 是   D: 的   E: 个   F: 好   G: 老师

208. I know him but I don't know his name.
    A: 他 B: 不 C: 的 D: 名字 E: 但是 F: 认识 G: 我 H: 知道 I: 他
    J: 我

209. The weather is very good, isn't it?
    A: 天气 B: 是 C: 吧 D: 非常 E: 好

210. Do you know his name?
    A: 知道 B: 的 C: 吗 D: 你 E: 名字 F: 他

211. Do you want to know?
    A: 想 B: 吗 C: 知道 D: 你

212. You can go wherever you like.
    A: 喜欢 B: 哪儿 C: 去 D: 您 E: 就 F: 去 G: 哪儿

213. I was busy when he called.
    A: 来 B: 时候 C: 他 D: 正在 E: 忙 F: 打电话 G: 我 H: 的

214. I know he's busy.
    A: 我 B: 忙 C: 知道 D: 他

215. It's nice to have friends.
    A: 有 B: 朋友 C: 真 D: 好

216. I don't know what that means.
    A: 什么 B: 意思 C: 我 D: 不 E: 是 F: 知道

HSK 2 GRAMMAR WORKBOOK   33

217. I don't know what you're trying to say.

　　A: 知道　B: 不　C: 我　D: 什么　E: 你　F: 说　G: 想

218. Do you know when she will come?

　　A: 吗　B: 什么　C: 她　D: 时候　E: 来　F: 知道　G: 你

219. Can you give me some tea?

　　A: 能　B: 点　C: 你　D: 给　E: 茶　F: 吗　G: 来　H: 我

220. I like dancing very much.

　　A: 我　B: 很　C: 喜欢　D: 跳舞

221. I'm starting to get cold.

　　A: 冷　B: 开始　C: 我　D: 了

222. This is my sister.

　　A: 的　B: 这　C: 是　D: 我　E: 妹妹

223. He doesn't know who I am.

　　A: 是　B: 我　C: 不　D: 他　E: 知道　F: 谁

224. I went into her room.

　　A: 她　B: 进　C: 了　D: 的　E: 我　F: 房间

225. Why are you asking me?

　　A: 我　B: 你　C: 为什么　D: 问

226. So we're all very busy.
    A: 非常 B: 我们 C: 都 D: 所以 E: 忙

227. I don't know what you think.
    A: 我 B: 怎么 C: 想 D: 不 E: 你 F: 知道

228. My husband and I are both teachers.
    A: 丈夫 B: 都 C: 我 D: 老师 E: 的 F: 和 G: 是 H: 我

229. I wonder if I wrote it correctly.
    A: 对 B: 不 C: 我 D: 不 E: 得 F: 对 G: 我 H: 写 I: 知道

230. Have you been busy since yesterday?
    A: 从 B: 忙 C: 就 D: 昨天 E: 你 F: 吗 G: 开始

231. I'd like to introduce you to him.
    A: 想 B: 他 C: 认识 D: 我 E: 你 F: 给 G: 介绍

232. I don't quite understand what you mean.
    A: 懂 B: 太 C: 的 D: 你 E: 不 F: 我 G: 意思 H: 听

233. Have you got home yet?
    A: 到 B: 了 C: 吗 D: 你 E: 已经 F: 家

234. How do you know that?
    A: 是 B: 你 C: 的 D: 怎么 E: 知道

235. Eat as much as you want.
A: 吃 B: 想 C: 就 D: 吃 E: 你 F: 多少 G: 多少

236. No one is in the room.
A: 在 B: 房间 C: 人 D: 里 E: 没有

237. Do you like singing?
A: 吗 B: 唱歌 C: 喜欢 D: 你

238. Do you know how to do it?
A: 知道 B: 做 C: 你 D: 怎么 E: 吗

239. Zero is in front of one.
A: 零 B: 在 C: 一 D: 前面

240. She doesn't know anyone because she's new here.
A: 谁 B: 她 C: 所以 D: 她 E: 的 F: 不 G: 认识 H: 都 I: 是 J: 新 K: 来 L: 因为

241. We're going to bed.
A: 睡觉 B: 我们 C: 要 D: 了

242. My sister is a teacher.
A: 是 B: 老师 C: 的 D: 妹妹 E: 我

243. That plane is really big.
A: 真 B: 那 C: 飞机 D: 大

244. We are at school together.
   A: 我们   B: 学校   C: 一起   D: 在

245. I know you like me.
   A: 我   B: 你   C: 喜欢   D: 我   E: 知道

246. Would you please let me have a moment
   A: 好   B: 你   C: 请   D: 吗   E: 让   F: 我   G: 一下

247. No one is going to look for you
   A: 人   B: 没有   C: 会   D: 你   E: 找

248. Do you know what we did?
   A: 了   B: 你   C: 吗   D: 什么   E: 我们   F: 知道   G: 做

249. Are you new here?
   A: 来   B: 的   C: 吗   D: 是   E: 新   F: 你

250. Does your husband like the child?
   A: 丈夫   B: 孩子   C: 的   D: 喜欢   E: 吗   F: 这个   G: 你

251. I know where he lives.
   A: 住   B: 我   C: 知道   D: 他   E: 哪儿

252. The food you cooked is delicious.
   A: 好吃   B: 真   C: 的   D: 做   E: 你   F: 菜

253. I hope he can come.
    A: 能 B: 来 C: 他 D: 我 E: 希望

254. What does she do in the evening?
    A: 晚上 B: 什么 C: 她 D: 做

255. Could you tell me how to get there, please?
    A: 走 B: 我 C: 请 D: 吗 E: 路 F: 好 G: 告诉 H: 怎么 I: 你

256. He bought me a watch.
    A: 买 B: 他 C: 我 D: 手表 E: 了 F: 给 G: 块

257. Give me something to drink.
    A: 给 B: 点 C: 我 D: 的 E: 喝

258. I know why you're happy.
    A: 你 B: 知道 C: 高兴 D: 为什么 E: 我

259. Who gave it to you?
    A: 那 B: 谁 C: 的 D: 给 E: 是 F: 你

260. I have a brother.
    A: 个 B: 哥哥 C: 我 D: 有

261. I don't know, and he doesn't know.
    A: 我 B: 知道 C: 他 D: 不 E: 也 F: 不 G: 知道

CHINESE SENTENCE STRUCTURE

262. I'm going to the restaurant.
A: 去   B: 要   C: 我   D: 饭店

263. Can you tell me what this is?
A: 你   B: 是   C: 我   D: 告诉   E: 能   F: 这   G: 吗   H: 什么

264. I want you to be ready.
A: 想   B: 我   C: 准备   D: 好   E: 你   F: 让

265. I know he's busy.
A: 我   B: 他   C: 知道   D: 忙   E: 很

266. He will be very busy tomorrow.
A: 很   B: 忙   C: 明天   D: 会   E: 他

267. What do you mean.
A: 什么   B: 你   C: 是   D: 意思

268. I think I'm right.
A: 对   B: 的   C: 我   D: 想   E: 是   F: 我

269. Everything I have to do has been done.
A: 的   B: 了   C: 已经   D: 都   E: 事情   F: 做   G: 要   H: 做   I: 我

270. You are taller than me.
A: 高   B: 还   C: 比   D: 你   E: 我

271. Why don't you know?
   A: 知道   B: 你   C: 为什么   D: 不

272. What a beautiful dress your sister is wearing today
   A: 啊   B: 的   C: 你   D: 多   E: 穿   F: 漂亮   G: 衣服   H: 今天   I: 妹妹

273. Do whatever you want.
   A: 你   B: 怎么   C: 做   D: 想   E: 就   F: 怎么   G: 做

274. I'm sorry I'm busy right now.
   A: 很   B: 对不起   C: 我   D: 现在   E: 忙

275. Your time is up.
   A: 时间   B: 你   C: 的   D: 到   E: 了

276. I don't like her either.
   A: 喜欢   B: 她   C: 我   D: 也   E: 不

277. Have you finished?
   A: 你   B: 做   C: 完   D: 吗   E: 了

278. She is much taller than me.
   A: 多   B: 得   C: 我   D: 高   E: 她   F: 比

279. No one knows where she is.
   A: 她   B: 知道   C: 在   D: 人   E: 哪儿   F: 没有

280. I don't know his name.
    A: 我   B: 不   C: 叫   D: 名字   E: 他   F: 知道   G: 什么

281. It is likely to rain today.
    A: 可能   B: 会   C: 下雨   D: 今天   E: 很

282. What kind of sports do you like?
    A: 运动   B: 什么   C: 喜欢   D: 你

283. Is your sister a student?
    A: 姐姐   B: 是   C: 吗   D: 你   E: 学生

284. Let's have a rest, shall we?
    A: 休息   B: 吗   C: 一下   D: 吧   E: 好   F: 我们

285. Do you have a cell phone?
    A: 有   B: 手机   C: 吗   D: 你

286. Do you have time in the morning?
    A: 时间   B: 吗   C: 你   D: 有   E: 上午

287. Could you wait a minute, please?
    A: 等   B: 吗   C: 你   D: 好   E: 请   F: 一下

288. Thank you for dancing with me.
    A: 跳舞   B: 你   C: 谢谢   D: 我   E: 和   F: 一起

289. Is he tall?

A: 长 B: 得 C: 高 D: 他 E: 吗

290. I don't quite understand what you mean.

A: 我 B: 您 C: 不 D: 太 E: 意思 F: 的 G: 懂

291. He spoke too fast.

A: 太 B: 说话 C: 快 D: 了 E: 他

292. What do you want to buy for him.

A: 买 B: 想 C: 什么 D: 给 E: 你 F: 他

293. He told me where to go.

A: 和 B: 我 C: 说 D: 了 E: 哪 F: 去 G: 要 H: 他

294. There is no one in the classroom.

A: 没有 B: 人 C: 里 D: 教室

295. That's tomorrow.

A: 吧 B: 是 C: 明天 D: 那

296. Do you know why the eyes are in front?

A: 在 B: 吗 C: 知道 D: 眼睛 E: 为什么 F: 前面 G: 长 H: 你

297. We all miss you very much.

A: 非常 B: 想 C: 你 D: 都 E: 我们

298. He may be in the classroom.
A: 他   B: 可能   C: 里   D: 教室   E: 在

299. Let's get started.
A: 开始   B: 让   C: 我们   D: 吧

300. I know I don't know anything.
A: 知道   B: 知道   C: 什么   D: 我   E: 不   F: 都   G: 我

301. Are you ready to get started?
A: 开始   B: 吗   C: 你   D: 准备   E: 好   F: 了

302. I want to know her name.
A: 名字   B: 她   C: 想   D: 知道   E: 我   F: 的

303. We know what we're doing.
A: 知道   B: 什么   C: 做   D: 我们   E: 我们   F: 在

304. Don't you feel cold?
A: 吗   B: 冷   C: 觉得   D: 你   E: 不

305. You don't have time.
A: 了   B: 你   C: 没有   D: 时间

306. Do you know where I live?
A: 住   B: 我   C: 哪   D: 知道   E: 你   F: 吗

HSK 2 GRAMMAR WORKBOOK

43

307. Let's go to the restaurant.
    A: 让   B: 去   C: 上   D: 我们   E: 饭馆

308. What are you looking for?
    A: 呢   B: 什么   C: 找   D: 在

309. I'm still studying.
    A: 还   B: 学习   C: 我   D: 在

310. Where were we？
    A: 我们   B: 说   C: 哪儿   D: 了   E: 到

311. He has gone.
    A: 走   B: 了   C: 他   D: 已经

312. I think I know who he is.
    A: 知道   B: 谁   C: 我   D: 想   E: 是   F: 他   G: 我

313. We told him something.
    A: 告诉   B: 我们   C: 他   D: 什么

314. Is your brother in good health?
    A: 身体   B: 哥哥   C: 你   D: 好   E: 吗

315. His sister is older than my brother.
    A: 我   B: 大   C: 比   D: 他   E: 姐姐   F: 哥哥

316. Would you like some more coffee?
    A: 点 B: 喝 C: 再 D: 你 E: 吗 F: 想 G: 咖啡

317. Now what do you want me to do?
    A: 你 B: 做 C: 现在 D: 我 E: 想 F: 让 G: 怎么

318. I'm from China.
    A: 我 B: 中国 C: 来 D: 的 E: 从

319. We are eating apples.
    A: 吃 B: 苹果 C: 我们 D: 正在

320. Tomorrow is my birthday.
    A: 是 B: 我 C: 生日 D: 明天

321. I know all about it.
    A: 知道 B: 都 C: 我 D: 了

322. I don't know what day he will come
    A: 几 B: 来 C: 不 D: 他 E: 星期 F: 知道 G: 我

323. I know you like coffee.
    A: 你 B: 喜欢 C: 知道 D: 咖啡 E: 我

324. I'm almost home.
    A: 就 B: 家 C: 了 D: 快 E: 到

325. Can you wait a minute?
    A: 一下   B: 吗   C: 等   D: 你   E: 可以

326. She played basketball with her father.
    A: 她   B: 爸爸   C: 打篮球   D: 和   E: 她

327. I'm in good health.
    A: 很   B: 好   C: 我   D: 身体

328. You can go when you like.
    A: 什么   B: 去   C: 时候   D: 时候   E: 就   F: 你   G: 去   H: 爱   I: 什么

329. What are you looking for?
    A: 什么   B: 在   C: 呢   D: 你   E: 找

330. It's better than having nothing.
    A: 比   B: 有   C: 没有   D: 好

331. The train station is by the side.
    A: 火车站   B: 就   C: 旁边   D: 在

332. There was no one in the room.
    A: 房间   B: 人   C: 里   D: 没有

333. She called her mother.
    A: 她   B: 她   C: 妈妈   D: 给   E: 打电话

334. I'm sleeping in my room.
   A: 房间   B: 在   C: 里   D: 睡觉   E: 我

335. Let us know when you will arrive.
   A: 知道   B: 我们   C: 什么   D: 让   E: 你   F: 到   G: 时候

336. I could do it without his help.
   A: 也   B: 没有   C: 我   D: 做   E: 能   F: 他   G: 帮助   H: 的

337. I'm looking for my friend.
   A: 找   B: 朋友   C: 我   D: 在   E: 我   F: 的

338. I'd love to go.
   A: 非常   B: 去   C: 想   D: 我

339. I don't know when we can eat.
   A: 可以   B: 我们   C: 什么   D: 知道   E: 我   F: 吃   G: 时候   H: 不

340. When do you start working?
   A: 你   B: 工作   C: 什么   D: 开始   E: 时候

341. Give me something to eat.
   A: 东西   B: 吃   C: 给   D: 我   E: 点

342. My dog is smaller than yours.
   A: 小   B: 狗   C: 比   D: 我   E: 你   F: 的   G: 的

343. I'm going by taxi.

   A: 要   B: 去   C: 出租车   D: 坐   E: 我

344. Tell me what you're thinking.

   A: 在   B: 我   C: 告诉   D: 什么   E: 想   F: 您

345. Let's get to work.

   A: 工作   B: 好   C: 我们   D: 开始   E: 吧

346. I still like you.

   A: 我   B: 喜欢   C: 你   D: 还

347. Mom, can I go swimming?

   A: 能   B: 妈妈   C: 吗   D: 游泳   E: 去   F: 我

348. Thank you for your help.

   A: 谢谢   B: 的   C: 给   D: 你   E: 帮助   F: 我

349. This is an egg.

   A: 是   B: 鸡蛋   C: 这   D: 个

350. Why are you so busy today?

   A: 为什么   B: 今天   C: 这么   D: 你   E: 忙

351. Please tell him to wait.

   A: 他   B: 请   C: 叫   D: 等   E: 一下

352. Would you like some coffee?
A: 喝 B: 吗 C: 要 D: 点 E: 咖啡 F: 你

353. Everyone knows me.
A: 大家 B: 都 C: 认识 D: 我

354. Would you like something to eat?
A: 什么 B: 想 C: 吗 D: 点 E: 吃 F: 您

355. Wear what you want.
A: 穿 B: 穿 C: 的 D: 想 E: 你

356. I may be wrong.
A: 错 B: 了 C: 我 D: 可能

357. She is not here, she is at work.
A: 不 B: 正在 C: 在 D: 她 E: 上班

358. What did you give me?
A: 了 B: 我 C: 给 D: 什么 E: 你

359. I drank milk.
A: 喝 B: 我 C: 了 D: 牛奶

360. Today is my birthday.
A: 我 B: 生日 C: 是 D: 的 E: 今天

HSK 2 GRAMMAR WORKBOOK

361. Has he come yet?
    A: 已经   B: 吗   C: 他   D: 来   E: 了

362. What else can you tell me?
    A: 告诉   B: 我   C: 你   D: 什么   E: 能   F: 还

363. Do you like watermelon?
    A: 吃   B: 喜欢   C: 你   D: 西瓜   E: 吗

364. We asked him what his name was.
    A: 名字   B: 他   C: 叫   D: 什么   E: 我们   F: 问

365. I know how to do it.
    A: 我   B: 怎么   C: 做   D: 知道

366. Can I go, too?
    A: 可以   B: 吗   C: 我   D: 也   E: 去

367. But not too much.
    A: 但是   B: 不   C: 太   D: 多

368. I'm going to the hospital.
    A: 要   B: 医院   C: 我   D: 去

369. Then I'll ask him tomorrow.
    A: 那   B: 他   C: 问   D: 我   E: 明天   F: 再

370. So he didn't go to school.
   A: 学校   B: 去   C: 所以   D: 没有   E: 他

371. What would you like to drink?
   A: 想   B: 什么   C: 您   D: 喝

372. I don't know why you don't like her.
   A: 她   B: 不   C: 我   D: 喜欢   E: 不   F: 为什么   G: 知道   H: 你

373. We're going to bed now.
   A: 现在   B: 要   C: 去   D: 我们   E: 睡觉

374. Do you have children already?
   A: 有   B: 吗   C: 已经   D: 你   E: 了   F: 孩子

375. You still don't sleep.
   A: 睡觉   B: 你   C: 还   D: 不

376. I know you're busy too.
   A: 忙   B: 很   C: 知道   D: 您   E: 我   F: 也

377. What were you doing this morning?
   A: 在   B: 什么   C: 今天   D: 你   E: 早上   F: 做

378. Where did you live last year?
   A: 你   B: 哪儿   C: 住   D: 在   E: 去年

379. Can I have a drink?
    A: 能   B: 我   C: 吗   D: 喝一杯

380. You know what I mean.
    A: 意思   B: 懂   C: 我   D: 的   E: 你

381. Just give me water, please.
    A: 给   B: 请   C: 就   D: 好   E: 了   F: 我   G: 水

382. We'll miss you when you're gone.
    A: 会   B: 的   C: 你   D: 走   E: 了   F: 你   G: 我们   H: 都   I: 想

383. The weather was very good yesterday.
    A: 昨天   B: 非常   C: 天气   D: 好

384. I'm going to say goodbye to you.
    A: 我   B: 说   C: 你   D: 和   E: 了   F: 要   G: 再见

385. I think he'll come.
    A: 吧   B: 会   C: 来   D: 我   E: 他   F: 的   G: 想

386. I'm reading a newspaper.
    A: 看   B: 正在   C: 报纸   D: 我

387. I don't know who he is.
    A: 我   B: 他   C: 知道   D: 不   E: 是   F: 谁

388. Work when it's time to work, rest when it's time for a break.
   A: 时候 B: 休息 C: 的 D: 的 E: 休息 F: 工作 G: 工作 H: 时候

389. Thank you for your help.
   A: 你 B: 帮助 C: 的 D: 谢谢

390. Excuse me, could you tell me the way to the railway station
   A: 怎么 B: 对不起 C: 请问 D: 火车站 E: 去 F: 走

391. I'll do whatever you ask me to do.
   A: 你 B: 做 C: 做 D: 我 E: 就 F: 什么 G: 什么 H: 让 I: 我

392. I didn't see it and you didn't see it.
   A: 没有 B: 看见 C: 看见 D: 你 E: 它 F: 它 G: 我 H: 没有 I: 也

393. I miss you very much.
   A: 非常 B: 我 C: 想 D: 你

394. Why are you here?
   A: 为什么 B: 你 C: 在 D: 这里

395. I don't love him anymore.
   A: 了 B: 已经 C: 我 D: 他 E: 不 F: 爱

396. Do you like coffee?
   A: 咖啡 B: 吗 C: 你 D: 喜欢

397. Another time

　　A: 吧　B: 时间　C: 再　D: 找

398. Did you call her?

　　A: 她　B: 打电话　C: 吗　D: 给　E: 你　F: 了

399. We know everything.

　　A: 什么　B: 知道　C: 都　D: 我们

400. Do you know what color she likes?

　　A: 什么　B: 你　C: 喜欢　D: 她　E: 吗　F: 颜色　G: 知道

401. Where's your room?

　　A: 哪　B: 的　C: 房间　D: 你　E: 在

402. Who asked her to come?

　　A: 她　B: 的　C: 让　D: 谁　E: 来

403. I don't know who she is.

　　A: 她　B: 我　C: 谁　D: 知道　E: 不　F: 是

404. Does he like noodles?

　　A: 面条　B: 喜欢　C: 吗　D: 他

405. I wish I had come yesterday

　　A: 我　B: 就　C: 了　D: 昨天　E: 来　F: 好

406. I don't know what to do.
   A: 不 B: 什么 C: 知道 D: 做 E: 要 F: 我

407. I know his name.
   A: 知道 B: 什么 C: 名字 D: 他 E: 我 F: 叫

408. Whose chair is this?
   A: 这 B: 是 C: 的 D: 椅子 E: 谁

409. Would you like some more noodles?
   A: 面条 B: 点 C: 你 D: 吗 E: 还 F: 吃 G: 再 H: 想

410. You are taller than her.
   A: 比 B: 高 C: 你 D: 要 E: 她

411. I'm not going anywhere.
   A: 哪儿 B: 也 C: 去 D: 不 E: 我

412. I don't know what the weather will be like tomorrow.
   A: 天气 B: 明天 C: 怎么样 D: 呢 E: 知道 F: 会 G: 不

413. I feel very happy.
   A: 我 B: 很 C: 快乐 D: 觉得

414. Eat what you want.
   A: 吃 B: 吧 C: 想 D: 什么 E: 吃 F: 什么 G: 就

415. I can help her.
   A: 帮助 B: 她 C: 能 D: 我

416. I don't know who's coming.

    A: 来   B: 不   C: 知道   D: 谁   E: 我   F: 要

417. Let's take a taxi.

    A: 吧   B: 出租车   C: 坐   D: 我们

418. I'm waiting for a taxi.

    A: 出租车   B: 我   C: 着   D: 等

419. Go to work. Bye.

    A: 去   B: 吧   C: 工作   D: 再见

420. We're still eating.

    A: 还   B: 呢   C: 吃   D: 我们   E: 在   F: 着

421. It is our job to help you.

    A: 的   B: 帮助   C: 工作   D: 你   E: 是   F: 我们

422. I'll go if you go.

    A: 你   B: 去   C: 就   D: 我   E: 去

423. Why don't you all say anything?

    A: 为什么   B: 都   C: 你们   D: 不   E: 说话

424. What did you do today?

    A: 什么   B: 今天   C: 您   D: 了   E: 做

425. He is a very good friend of mine.
    A: 的 B: 我 C: 朋友 D: 非常 E: 他 F: 是 G: 好

426. Let's go by bus.
    A: 坐 B: 去 C: 让 D: 我们 E: 公共汽车

427. What did he say to you?
    A: 他 B: 了 C: 你 D: 什么 E: 对 F: 说 G: 些

428. Coffee is cold.
    A: 咖啡 B: 的 C: 冷 D: 是

429. Do you like snow?
    A: 雪 B: 你 C: 吗 D: 喜欢

430. Come on, let's go together.
    A: 来 B: 我们 C: 去 D: 吧 E: 一起

431. I don't like tea or coffee.
    A: 不 B: 不 C: 茶 D: 喜欢 E: 我 F: 也 G: 咖啡 H: 喜欢

432. He waited a long time.
    A: 等 B: 很 C: 长 D: 了 E: 他 F: 的 G: 时间

433. He doesn't listen to me.
    A: 他 B: 不 C: 我 D: 说话 E: 听

434. I don't know where he is.
   A: 我   B: 不   C: 哪   D: 在   E: 知道   F: 他

435. I hope you can come and work with me.
   A: 我   B: 一起   C: 工作   D: 来   E: 和   F: 能   G: 希望   H: 我   I: 你

436. He also studies Chinese.
   A: 他   B: 汉语   C: 学习   D: 也

437. Whose fault is it?
   A: 的   B: 是   C: 呢   D: 谁   E: 错

438. What are you thinking?
   A: 想   B: 你   C: 正在   D: 什么

439. All right, let's go.
   A: 走   B: 我们   C: 吧   D: 吧   E: 好

440. He asked me if I was happy.
   A: 他   B: 问   C: 不   D: 我   E: 快   F: 快乐

441. He is making noodles.
   A: 正在   B: 他   C: 面条   D: 做

442. Do whatever you want.
   A: 想   B: 做   C: 就   D: 什么   E: 做   F: 什么   G: 你

443. Fish is cheap today.
   A: 便宜   B: 今天   C: 很   D: 鱼

444. Please come to the front.
   A: 来   B: 到   C: 请   D: 前面

445. What would you like to eat?
   A: 什么   B: 您   C: 想   D: 吃

446. We'll start when he comes
   A: 开始   B: 就   C: 来   D: 了   E: 他   F: 我们

447. What did he ask you
   A: 他   B: 你   C: 什么   D: 问

448. Let's ask the teacher.
   A: 老师   B: 让   C: 问   D: 我们

449. He'll be my sister's good husband.
   A: 我   B: 的   C: 丈夫   D: 他   E: 妹妹   F: 会   G: 是   H: 好   I: 的

450. I know you are a teacher.
   A: 是   B: 我   C: 你   D: 老师   E: 知道

451. He will be very busy next month.
   A: 会   B: 很   C: 下个月   D: 忙   E: 他

452. Where is your watch?
    A: 在 B: 哪儿 C: 你 D: 手表 E: 的

453. He'll be a good husband.
    A: 会 B: 他 C: 个 D: 的 E: 是 F: 丈夫 G: 好

454. How much does it cost?
    A: 钱 B: 这 C: 多少 D: 要

455. Let's go get something to eat.
    A: 去 B: 点 C: 吧 D: 吃 E: 东西

456. Who is your brother?
    A: 你 B: 哥哥 C: 谁 D: 是

457. Do you know what he said?
    A: 了 B: 知道 C: 吗 D: 你 E: 他 F: 说 G: 什么

458. When are you going?
    A: 你 B: 什么 C: 时候 D: 去

459. Would you like some coffee?
    A: 点 B: 吗 C: 喝 D: 咖啡

460. I'll do it tomorrow.
    A: 我 B: 做 C: 再 D: 明天

461. Where's your sister?
    A: 的   B: 妹妹   C: 呢   D: 你

462. I think it's you.
    A: 你   B: 是   C: 觉得   D: 我

463. We'll leave as soon as you're ready.
    A: 我们   B: 准备   C: 走   D: 好   E: 一   F: 就   G: 你

464. I don't like it either.
    A: 也   B: 不   C: 喜欢   D: 我

465. She doesn't like her husband.
    A: 的   B: 不   C: 她   D: 喜欢   E: 她   F: 丈夫

466. My sister has a job.
    A: 工作   B: 的   C: 我   D: 姐姐   E: 有

467. We have too much work to do.
    A: 要   B: 多   C: 了   D: 做   E: 我们   F: 太   G: 的   H: 工作

468. My son is taller than me.
    A: 我   B: 比   C: 我   D: 儿子   E: 高

469. Can you ask her to call me?
    A: 给   B: 她   C: 吗   D: 能   E: 我   F: 打电话   G: 你   H: 让

HSK 2 GRAMMAR WORKBOOK

470. Can I help you?

   A: 你   B: 帮助   C: 可以   D: 吗   E: 我

471. You're not busy, are you?

   A: 忙   B: 不   C: 你   D: 吧   E: 对

472. I don't like him either.

   A: 也   B: 我   C: 他   D: 喜欢   E: 不

473. When are you leaving?

   A: 走   B: 你   C: 什么   D: 时候

474. I know who he is.

   A: 他   B: 我   C: 谁   D: 是   E: 知道

475. What's your favorite fruit?

   A: 您   B: 喜欢   C: 水果   D: 什么   E: 最

476. I don't have time now.

   A: 时间   B: 现在   C: 我   D: 没有

477. I was ill yesterday.

   A: 生病   B: 昨天   C: 我   D: 了

478. I think we can be good friends.

   A: 做好   B: 觉得   C: 我   D: 朋友   E: 可以   F: 我们

479. It's a matter of time.
    A: 这 B: 时间 C: 问题 D: 个 E: 是

480. He began to look for a job.
    A: 开始 B: 工作 C: 他 D: 找 E: 了

481. Noodles and rice are delicious.
    A: 都 B: 和 C: 好吃 D: 很 E: 米饭 F: 面条

482. Do you like swimming?
    A: 游泳 B: 喜欢 C: 你 D: 吗

483. I'm at the railway station.
    A: 到 B: 我 C: 了 D: 火车站

484. I don't like eggs.
    A: 鸡蛋 B: 吃 C: 喜欢 D: 不 E: 我

485. I'm right behind you.
    A: 就 B: 你 C: 后面 D: 在 E: 我

486. What color is your dress?
    A: 是 B: 的 C: 颜色 D: 什么 E: 衣服 F: 你

487. We'll start tomorrow morning.
    A: 上午 B: 开始 C: 我们 D: 明天

488. How to read your last name.

   A: 的   B: 怎么   C: 你   D: 读   E: 姓

489. Why do you like me?

   A: 你   B: 我   C: 为什么   D: 喜欢

490. You can read the book.

   A: 可以   B: 你   C: 这   D: 书   E: 看

491. I don't like watermelon.

   A: 喜欢   B: 西瓜   C: 吃   D: 我   E: 不

492. I don't know when he will come.

   A: 他   B: 什么   C: 不   D: 时候   E: 来   F: 知道

493. He probably knows I like him.

   A: 可能   B: 我   C: 喜欢   D: 知道   E: 他   F: 很   G: 他

494. You may be right.

   A: 是   B: 的   C: 对   D: 你   E: 可能

495. What's the problem?

   A: 什么   B: 有   C: 吗   D: 问题

496. He may not be happy.

   A: 不   B: 高兴   C: 他   D: 可能

497. Your watch is more expensive than mine.
    A: 我 B: 比 C: 的 D: 手表 E: 你 F: 贵 G: 的

498. Mother said I was talking too fast.
    A: 太 B: 妈妈 C: 我 D: 快 E: 说话 F: 说

499. That's what we want to know.
    A: 这 B: 的 C: 想 D: 就是 E: 知道 F: 我们

500. She told me that her mother had bought it for her.
    A: 我 B: 了 C: 她 D: 她 E: 告诉 F: 妈妈 G: 给 H: 买 I: 她

501. Are you going, too?
    A: 你 B: 也 C: 要 D: 吗 E: 去

502. You can have a rest tomorrow.
    A: 明天 B: 休息 C: 可以 D: 你 E: 就

503. I know what it is.
    A: 是 B: 知道 C: 我 D: 什么 E: 那

504. Would you like to eat with us?
    A: 我们 B: 一起 C: 你 D: 和 E: 吗 F: 吃

505. He likes reading newspapers.
    A: 看 B: 喜欢 C: 他 D: 报纸

HSK 2 GRAMMAR WORKBOOK   65

506. I think he is a doctor.
    A: 觉得   B: 我   C: 医生   D: 是   E: 他

507. Your father is very tall.
    A: 你   B: 爸爸   C: 很   D: 高

508. Our restaurant is better than that one.
    A: 比   B: 那   C: 好   D: 饭店   E: 的   F: 家   G: 我们   H: 饭店

509. I feel very busy at work.
    A: 我   B: 觉得   C: 工作   D: 忙   E: 很

510. Do you feel tired?
    A: 累   B: 觉得   C: 吗   D: 你

511. No one can know.
    A: 人   B: 没有   C: 知道   D: 能

512. Why should I give him money?
    A: 他   B: 钱   C: 我   D: 要   E: 为什么   F: 给

513. Is this for sale
    A: 的   B: 吗   C: 这   D: 要   E: 东西   F: 是   G: 卖

514. Do you feel better now?
    A: 了   B: 你   C: 吗   D: 觉得   E: 好   F: 现在   G: 点

515. You can do it when you have time

    A: 吧   B: 做   C: 再   D: 时间   E: 有   F: 你

516. I'm not as tall as you.

    A: 没有   B: 我   C: 你   D: 高

517. You're not right.

    A: 你   B: 不   C: 说   D: 得   E: 对

518. Are you busy now?

    A: 现在   B: 吗   C: 忙   D: 你

519. Did you call me in the evening?

    A: 我   B: 您   C: 晚上   D: 打电话   E: 给   F: 了   G: 吗

520. She likes good food.

    A: 喜欢   B: 的   C: 东西   D: 她   E: 好吃

521. You have too many questions.

    A: 了   B: 太   C: 问题   D: 多   E: 你

522. The doctor prescribed me medicine.

    A: 给   B: 药   C: 我   D: 医生   E: 了   F: 开

523. I'm waiting for my friend.

    A: 的   B: 等   C: 朋友   D: 在   E: 我   F: 我

HSK 2 GRAMMAR WORKBOOK 67

524. Can you tell me where I was wrong
    A: 可以 B: 我 C: 吗 D: 在 E: 告诉 F: 你 G: 错 H: 哪儿 I: 我

525. She told me that she knew my brother.
    A: 我 B: 她 C: 告诉 D: 哥哥 E: 我 F: 的 G: 认识 H: 她

526. Tomorrow is her birthday.
    A: 的 B: 生日 C: 她 D: 是 E: 明天

527. I'm new here.
    A: 是 B: 我 C: 的 D: 新 E: 来

528. Let's go when you want to.
    A: 你 B: 走 C: 就 D: 想 E: 走 F: 时候 G: 吧 H: 的

529. You can also have some rice.
    A: 吃 B: 你 C: 米饭 D: 点 E: 可以 F: 还

530. No one knows his real name.
    A: 知道 B: 没有 C: 他 D: 的 E: 名字 F: 真 G: 人

531. Can I not come for tomorrow's class?
    A: 我 B: 吗 C: 课 D: 明天 E: 来 F: 不 G: 能 H: 的

532. Can it be cheaper?
    A: 便宜 B: 吗 C: 可以 D: 点

533. Can I ask you a question?
A: 你 B: 问题 C: 吗 D: 问 E: 个 F: 可以 G: 我

534. Let's go to the hospital now.
A: 就 B: 医院 C: 去 D: 现在 E: 吧 F: 我们

535. It's time for you to get your tea ready.
A: 茶 B: 准备 C: 好 D: 是 E: 时候 F: 你 G: 的 H: 了

536. My father told you where he had gone.
A: 他 B: 了 C: 爸爸 D: 我 E: 去 F: 你 G: 哪儿 H: 告诉

537. That's my favorite chair.
A: 喜欢 B: 那 C: 最 D: 的 E: 我 F: 是 G: 椅子

538. I'll be busy tomorrow.
A: 很 B: 我 C: 忙 D: 会 E: 明天

539. We don't know if he will come or not.
A: 他 B: 来 C: 不 D: 不 E: 来 F: 知道 G: 我们

540. I know I did something wrong.
A: 我 B: 我 C: 知道 D: 做 E: 了 F: 错

541. He is very funny.
A: 笑 B: 他 C: 很 D: 会 E: 说

HSK 2 GRAMMAR WORKBOOK 69

542. Are you leaving now?
   A: 了 B: 吗 C: 你 D: 要 E: 走 F: 已经

543. Eat whatever you want.
   A: 就 B: 什么 C: 想 D: 吃 E: 吃 F: 什么 G: 你

544. I know you still love me.
   A: 知道 B: 还 C: 我 D: 你 E: 我 F: 爱

545. He may like his work.
   A: 工作 B: 他 C: 他 D: 可能 E: 喜欢 F: 的

546. Do you know my name?
   A: 吗 B: 名字 C: 的 D: 你 E: 知道 F: 我

547. I'll wait for you in front of the school.
   A: 我 B: 前面 C: 学校 D: 等 E: 你 F: 在

548. I don't have time for rest.
   A: 的 B: 休息 C: 时间 D: 没有 E: 我

549. I'm not going anywhere.
   A: 不 B: 去 C: 哪 D: 也 E: 我

550. It was very cold this morning.
   A: 冷 B: 今天 C: 非常 D: 早上

551. I don't understand at all.
   A: 一点儿 B: 懂 C: 都 D: 不 E: 我

552. I'm looking for a job.
   A: 在 B: 工作 C: 我 D: 找

553. I don't know her and I don't know who she is.
   A: 谁 B: 不 C: 她 D: 不 E: 认识 F: 我 G: 也 H: 是 I: 她 J: 知道
   K: 我

554. Are you talking to me?
   A: 吗 B: 是 C: 对 D: 在 E: 我 F: 说 G: 你

555. He asked me to do it and I did it.
   A: 了 B: 做 C: 让 D: 做 E: 他 F: 我 G: 就 H: 我

556. My sister is older than my brother.
   A: 我 B: 哥哥 C: 姐姐 D: 我 E: 大 F: 比

557. He likes his school very much.
   A: 他 B: 学校 C: 他 D: 喜欢 E: 的 F: 非常

558. I like traveling very much.
   A: 喜欢 B: 我 C: 旅游 D: 很

559. She gave him some hot drinks.
   A: 了 B: 的 C: 他 D: 热 E: 些 F: 给 G: 喝 H: 她

HSK 2 GRAMMAR WORKBOOK

560. I also want to go to Beijing.
   A: 我   B: 去   C: 北京   D: 想   E: 也

561. He loves her and she loves him.
   A: 她   B: 他   C: 她   D: 爱   E: 他   F: 也   G: 爱

562. Our classroom is very small.
   A: 的   B: 教室   C: 非常   D: 我们   E: 小

563. She sings very well.
   A: 好   B: 非常   C: 唱歌   D: 她

564. He walks very slowly.
   A: 得   B: 慢   C: 他   D: 非常   E: 走

565. But I don't have any money.
   A: 我   B: 钱   C: 没有   D: 但是

566. Thank you for coming to the railway station to see me off.
   A: 我   B: 火车站   C: 你   D: 来   E: 谢谢   F: 送

567. Give me your cell phone.
   A: 给   B: 手机   C: 我   D: 你   E: 的

568. I think you'll like it, too.
   A: 也   B: 你   C: 喜欢   D: 会   E: 的   F: 我   G: 想

569. Its color is red.
   A: 红 B: 的 C: 是 D: 颜色 E: 的 F: 它

570. I'm glad I can help you.
   A: 很 B: 你 C: 帮助 D: 能 E: 高兴 F: 我 G: 我

571. I'm your sister.
   A: 妹妹 B: 我 C: 的 D: 是 E: 你

572. I'm going to bed.
   A: 要 B: 睡觉 C: 了 D: 我

573. Do you have any children?
   A: 有 B: 吗 C: 你 D: 孩子

574. That's my problem.
   A: 问题 B: 这 C: 的 D: 我 E: 是

575. There is a good chance that it will rain tomorrow.
   A: 下雨 B: 可能 C: 有 D: 明天 E: 很

576. I have a brother.
   A: 有 B: 弟弟 C: 我 D: 个

577. Let me have a look at what you bought.
   A: 让 B: 买 C: 一下 D: 的 E: 我 F: 东西 G: 你 H: 看

HSK 2 GRAMMAR WORKBOOK

578. I think what you are doing is wrong.

    A: 的   B: 正在   C: 我   D: 做   E: 觉得   F: 你   G: 错   H: 的   I: 是

579. Where's everybody?

    A: 大家   B: 哪儿   C: 都   D: 在

580. I'll call as soon as I get to the airport.

    A: 机场   B: 打电话   C: 给   D: 我   E: 到   F: 就   G: 一   H: 你

581. We are all tired.

    A: 了   B: 都   C: 累   D: 我们

582. No one listens to me.

    A: 我   B: 听   C: 没有   D: 人   E: 说话

583. When do you get up in the morning?

    A: 什么   B: 早上   C: 时候   D: 你   E: 起床

584. I think you're right.

    A: 是   B: 对   C: 我   D: 认为   E: 的   F: 你

585. Can you tell me how to get to the railway station?

    A: 吗   B: 我   C: 告诉   D: 火车站   E: 怎么   F: 去   G: 能   H: 你

586. He looked at his watch.

    A: 看   B: 手表   C: 他   D: 看   E: 了

587. Can you not tell him?

A: 你 B: 能 C: 不能不 D: 他 E: 告诉

588. I know what you did.

A: 了 B: 做 C: 什么 D: 知道 E: 你 F: 我

589. I go shopping every morning.

A: 东西 B: 买 C: 我 D: 去 E: 都 F: 每天 G: 早上

590. Tell me when to start.

A: 我 B: 开始 C: 告诉 D: 时候 E: 什么

591. I don't know what it is.

A: 我 B: 是 C: 什么 D: 知道 E: 不 F: 那

592. Do you still know me?

A: 我 B: 吗 C: 还 D: 你 E: 认识

593. Has the film begun?

A: 已经 B: 吗 C: 电影 D: 了 E: 开始

594. I want him to wait for me.

A: 我 B: 我 C: 等 D: 要 E: 他

595. I like snow very much.

A: 很 B: 我 C: 雪 D: 喜欢

596. You know what I want to hear.
    A: 想   B: 听   C: 你   D: 知道   E: 我   F: 什么

597. I don't like eggs.
    A: 鸡蛋   B: 喜欢   C: 不   D: 我

598. I'd like some fish.
    A: 想   B: 我   C: 鱼   D: 点   E: 吃

599. Do you like fish?
    A: 鱼   B: 吗   C: 你   D: 喜欢   E: 吃

600. Are you a student here?
    A: 您   B: 的   C: 吗   D: 是   E: 学生   F: 这里

601. Can you give it to me?
    A: 你   B: 能   C: 给   D: 吗   E: 我

602. Can you come here
    A: 吗   B: 来   C: 一下   D: 能   E: 你

603. I bought it cheap.
    A: 买   B: 东西   C: 很   D: 这   E: 我   F: 得   G: 便宜

604. I'm tired now.
    A: 累   B: 我   C: 很   D: 现在

605. She told me she liked you.

　　A: 你　B: 说　C: 她　D: 她　E: 对　F: 喜欢　G: 我

606. Hey, are you still here?

　　A: 在　B: 喂　C: 吗　D: 还　E: 你

607. I'm tired.

　　A: 已经　B: 我　C: 累　D: 了

608. Why do the eyes grow in front?

　　A: 前面　B: 眼睛　C: 在　D: 长　E: 为什么

609. My dog is white.

　　A: 白　B: 我　C: 的　D: 的　E: 狗　F: 是

610. Seven is two less than nine

　　A: 二　B: 少　C: 七　D: 九　E: 比

611. Do you want to play basketball?

　　A: 想　B: 打篮球　C: 你　D: 去　E: 吗

612. Why don't you take a break?

　　A: 为什么　B: 不　C: 一下　D: 你　E: 休息

613. I hope he will wait for me.

　　A: 等　B: 他　C: 我　D: 会　E: 我　F: 希望

HSK 2 GRAMMAR WORKBOOK

614. She may not be coming.
    A: 可能 B: 不 C: 来 D: 了 E: 她

615. What's wrong with you?
    A: 有 B: 什么 C: 你 D: 问题

616. This is my favorite.
    A: 这 B: 喜欢 C: 最 D: 我 E: 的 F: 是

617. Your eyes are so beautiful.
    A: 的 B: 漂亮 C: 眼睛 D: 真 E: 你

618. Will he tell me what I really want?
    A: 吗 B: 会 C: 真正 D: 什么 E: 我 F: 告诉 G: 他 H: 我 I: 想要

619. Did you run?
    A: 跑步 B: 了 C: 你 D: 吗

620. I like to be with you.
    A: 喜欢 B: 我 C: 在 D: 和 E: 一起 F: 你

621. You know what I mean?
    A: 懂 B: 你 C: 意思 D: 的 E: 吗 F: 我

622. Do you have a pencil?
    A: 吗 B: 你 C: 有 D: 铅笔

623. I'm your friend, right?

A: 对   B: 是   C: 朋友   D: 你   E: 我   F: 吗   G: 的

624. We can walk together.

A: 可以   B: 走   C: 一起   D: 我们

625. He may come tomorrow afternoon.

A: 下午   B: 他   C: 来   D: 可能   E: 明天

626. I asked you what you were thinking.

A: 想   B: 什么   C: 问   D: 你   E: 在   F: 我

627. We're good friends, right?

A: 吧   B: 对   C: 是   D: 朋友   E: 好   F: 我们

628. I told you to go. Why didn't you go?

A: 你   B: 叫   C: 为什么   D: 去   E: 我   F: 不   G: 你   H: 去

629. He's next to her.

A: 的   B: 她   C: 旁边   D: 在   E: 他

630. Would you like some coffee?

A: 咖啡   B: 你   C: 喝   D: 点   E: 想   F: 吗

631. How could you not know.

A: 不   B: 知道   C: 怎么   D: 你   E: 会

HSK 2 GRAMMAR WORKBOOK 79

632. Where's your sister?
   A: 姐姐   B: 你   C: 呢   D: 的

633. Can you tell me where you live?
   A: 住   B: 我   C: 哪儿   D: 能   E: 告诉   F: 你   G: 你

634. My mother asked me to take some medicine.
   A: 我   B: 我   C: 吃   D: 点   E: 妈妈   F: 让   G: 药

635. I'll call you tomorrow morning.
   A: 上午   B: 给   C: 明天   D: 我   E: 你   F: 打电话

636. Do you want to sing?
   A: 吗   B: 你   C: 唱歌   D: 要

637. We are going to dance tomorrow.
   A: 我们   B: 要   C: 去   D: 跳舞   E: 明天

638. You're not going, are you?
   A: 准备   B: 吗   C: 你   D: 去   E: 不   F: 是

639. Well, I get it. Thank you.
   A: 谢谢   B: 你   C: 好   D: 我   E: 懂   F: 吧   G: 了

640. I'll come tomorrow evening.
   A: 来   B: 明天   C: 晚上   D: 我

641. He didn't like her in the first place.
   A: 一   B: 开始   C: 不   D: 就   E: 喜欢   F: 她   G: 他

642. Are you at work?
   A: 你   B: 在   C: 上班   D: 吗

643. I know I was wrong.
   A: 我   B: 知道   C: 了   D: 错   E: 我

644. Sell it to us?
   A: 我们   B: 卖   C: 给   D: 吧

645. It may rain.
   A: 可能   B: 下雨   C: 要   D: 了

646. I like coffee very much.
   A: 喜欢   B: 我   C: 咖啡   D: 非常

647. Everyone knows her.
   A: 大家   B: 认识   C: 都   D: 她

648. He said he loved me too.
   A: 爱   B: 说   C: 他   D: 也   E: 他   F: 我   G: 了

649. I hope you'll like it.
   A: 会   B: 希望   C: 它   D: 你   E: 我   F: 喜欢

HSK 2 GRAMMAR WORKBOOK   81

650. How about looking for a job?

　　A: 去　B: 怎么样　C: 工作　D: 找

651. He asked the teacher why he let him go to the cinema.

　　A: 让　B: 问　C: 电影　D: 看　E: 他　F: 老师　G: 为什么　H: 他

652. I don't think she is beautiful.

　　A: 她　B: 不　C: 我　D: 漂亮　E: 觉得

653. I know her sister.

　　A: 妹妹　B: 认识　C: 我　D: 她　E: 的

654. My birthday is coming up.

　　A: 到　B: 就　C: 快　D: 的　E: 了　F: 生日　G: 我

655. I'd like to know her name.

　　A: 很　B: 我　C: 知道　D: 想　E: 的　F: 名字　G: 她

656. Now who's laughing?

　　A: 笑　B: 在　C: 现在　D: 谁

657. I can start tomorrow.

　　A: 开始　B: 明天　C: 我　D: 可以

658. When did you start playing basketball?

　　A: 你　B: 的　C: 开始　D: 时候　E: 打篮球　F: 什么

659. It is likely to rain tomorrow.
    A: 下雨 B: 有 C: 明天 D: 可能 E: 会

660. I think your job is OK
    A: 工作 B: 觉得 C: 你 D: 还 E: 可以 F: 的 G: 我

661. Her father is very tall.
    A: 爸爸 B: 高 C: 很 D: 她

662. Why don't you call me?
    A: 给 B: 不 C: 我 D: 为什么 E: 你 F: 打电话

663. Do what I tell you to do
    A: 叫 B: 怎么 C: 做 D: 你 E: 就 F: 你 G: 怎么 H: 做 I: 我

664. I like you very much.
    A: 喜欢 B: 非常 C: 我 D: 你

665. You can go now.
    A: 您 B: 可以 C: 走 D: 了

666. I hope this is right.
    A: 对 B: 我 C: 这 D: 希望 E: 的 F: 是

667. Why don't you say anything?
    A: 为什么 B: 你 C: 不 D: 说话

668. It'll be all right tomorrow.

   A: 好 B: 明天 C: 会 D: 的

669. I don't know when he can come.

   A: 时候 B: 什么 C: 来 D: 我 E: 知道 F: 不 G: 他 H: 能

670. She is looking for a job.

   A: 找 B: 她 C: 在 D: 工作

671. I'll have some noodles.

   A: 吃 B: 我 C: 面条 D: 点

672. It was raining when we arrived.

   A: 到 B: 正在 C: 的 D: 时候 E: 我们 F: 下雨

673. Your friends will miss you.

   A: 您 B: 朋友 C: 的 D: 您 E: 的 F: 想 G: 会

674. He can read very well.

   A: 读 B: 他 C: 得 D: 好 E: 能 F: 很

675. What else did he say?

   A: 还 B: 他 C: 说 D: 什么 E: 了

676. I'm going to have a Chinese class.

   A: 上 B: 汉语 C: 我 D: 去 E: 课

677. Will you tell me?
A: 吗 B: 你 C: 能 D: 告诉 E: 我

678. You're a son, too.
A: 个 B: 是 C: 你 D: 儿子 E: 也

679. What do you want to know?
A: 你 B: 想 C: 些 D: 知道 E: 什么

680. Please call me.
A: 请 B: 我 C: 给 D: 打电话

681. So what are we going to do?
A: 做 B: 那 C: 我们 D: 要 E: 什么

682. I know you will.
A: 我 B: 你 C: 知道 D: 的 E: 会

683. She also studies Chinese.
A: 也 B: 汉语 C: 学习 D: 她

684. I watched TV this morning.
A: 了 B: 今天 C: 我 D: 电视 E: 看 F: 早上

685. What's your favorite color?
A: 喜欢 B: 是 C: 的 D: 你 E: 什么 F: 颜色 G: 最

HSK 2 GRAMMAR WORKBOOK

686. Please tell me how to get to the airport.

    A: 我   B: 机场   C: 你   D: 告诉   E: 去   F: 请   G: 怎么

687. When will she get home?

    A: 到   B: 什么   C: 她   D: 家   E: 时候

688. You did very well.

    A: 很   B: 得   C: 做   D: 好   E: 你

689. I don't know anything.

    A: 不   B: 都   C: 知道   D: 我   E: 什么

690. He did nothing wrong.

    A: 他   B: 做   C: 没有   D: 错

691. Let me have a look at your ticket.

    A: 你   B: 看   C: 票   D: 我   E: 的   F: 让   G: 一下

692. What are you doing?

    A: 正在   B: 你   C: 做   D: 什么

693. Fish and mutton are not delicious together.

    A: 在   B: 好吃   C: 一起   D: 鱼   E: 羊肉   F: 和   G: 不

694. Why don't you listen?

    A: 为什么   B: 不   C: 听   D: 你

695. This is for you.
    A: 这 B: 你 C: 给 D: 是 E: 的

696. I want to go with you.
    A: 和 B: 走 C: 我 D: 你 E: 想 F: 一起

697. I don't know.
    A: 不 B: 我 C: 也 D: 知道

698. Let's have a rest.
    A: 休息 B: 一下 C: 吧 D: 我们

699. She went into the room.
    A: 她 B: 房间 C: 了 D: 进

700. But my birthday is tomorrow.
    A: 明天 B: 就 C: 的 D: 在 E: 生日 F: 但是 G: 我

701. I'll call you tomorrow.
    A: 打电话 B: 给 C: 我 D: 你 E: 会 F: 明天

702. I love her and she loves me.
    A: 我 B: 爱 C: 爱 D: 也 E: 我 F: 她 G: 她

703. Do you have a ticket for today?
    A: 票 B: 吗 C: 有 D: 的 E: 你 F: 今天

704. I'm at the airport now.

A: 现在   B: 我   C: 机场   D: 在

705. I saw her swimming.

A: 她   B: 我   C: 看见   D: 游泳   E: 在

706. I don't have any money.

A: 钱   B: 没有   C: 一点儿   D: 也   E: 我

707. How many apples do you want?

A: 要   B: 个   C: 多少   D: 你   E: 苹果

708. When can we eat?

A: 时候   B: 什么   C: 吃饭   D: 可以   E: 我们

709. We all like you very much.

A: 你   B: 喜欢   C: 我们   D: 都   E: 非常

710. We don't know much about you.

A: 我们   B: 得   C: 不   D: 你   E: 对   F: 知道   G: 多

711. What do you want to hear now?

A: 要   B: 些   C: 听   D: 现在   E: 什么   F: 你

712. What's my room number?

A: 的   B: 号码   C: 多少   D: 房间   E: 是   F: 我

713. My home is close to the school.
    A: 学校   B: 我   C: 很   D: 离   E: 的   F: 近   G: 家

714. Can I come to your class?
    A: 我   B: 吗   C: 你   D: 的   E: 来   F: 可以   G: 听   H: 课

715. Do you know where he lives?
    A: 知道   B: 哪儿   C: 吗   D: 住   E: 他   F: 你

716. Does she know you?
    A: 吗   B: 你   C: 她   D: 知道

717. Looking for something?
    A: 吗   B: 东西   C: 找   D: 在

718. I don't know where you're going.
    A: 我   B: 哪   C: 知道   D: 去   E: 你   F: 不   G: 要

719. Wherever you want to go, we'll go.
    A: 去   B: 哪儿   C: 就   D: 你   E: 我们   F: 爱   G: 去   H: 哪儿

720. My Chinese teacher is a man.
    A: 男   B: 汉语   C: 我   D: 是   E: 的   F: 老师

721. I'm not busy right now.
    A: 我   B: 不   C: 现在   D: 忙

HSK 2 GRAMMAR WORKBOOK

722. Let's go to school together.
　　A: 我们　B: 学校　C: 一起　D: 去

723. I'm busy right now.
　　A: 很　B: 现在　C: 忙　D: 我

724. Can I call you tomorrow?
　　A: 可以　B: 你　C: 明天　D: 我　E: 吗　F: 给　G: 打电话

725. I'm tired let's go to bed.
　　A: 让　B: 睡觉　C: 了　D: 我们　E: 吧　F: 我　G: 累

726. When will you get up tomorrow?
　　A: 你　B: 起床　C: 什么　D: 时候　E: 明天

727. I like it very much.
　　A: 非常　B: 我　C: 喜欢　D: 它

728. I'm tired after class.
　　A: 我　B: 很　C: 累　D: 了　E: 上　F: 课　G: 完

729. Could you please write it down?
　　A: 写　B: 你　C: 它　D: 把　E: 下来　F: 能　G: 吗

730. Something went into my eyes.
　　A: 眼睛　B: 有　C: 进入　D: 的　E: 我　F: 东西

731. I was not busy yesterday.
    A: 我   B: 忙   C: 昨天   D: 不

732. What do you think of the rice?
    A: 米饭   B: 这   C: 觉得   D: 你   E: 怎么样

733. Let's go to bed.
    A: 去   B: 吧   C: 我们   D: 睡觉

734. I think you're tired.
    A: 累   B: 你   C: 我   D: 觉得

735. It's ok, I can wait.
    A: 我   B: 可以   C: 等   D: 没关系

736. The plane is ready.
    A: 飞机   B: 好   C: 准备   D: 了

737. He told me that she was ill.
    A: 我   B: 他   C: 生病   D: 告诉   E: 她   F: 了

738. I probably ate the most.
    A: 得   B: 最   C: 可能   D: 多   E: 我   F: 吃

739. Can I go now?
    A: 我   B: 可以   C: 现在   D: 走   E: 吗   F: 了

HSK 2 GRAMMAR WORKBOOK

740. Give her some time.
    A: 给   B: 点   C: 她   D: 时间

741. Do you like noodles?
    A: 爱   B: 你   C: 面条   D: 吃   E: 吗

742. I know you're right.
    A: 的   B: 是   C: 你   D: 我   E: 对   F: 知道

743. But you have children.
    A: 但是   B: 你   C: 孩子   D: 有

744. Mother made me a new dress.
    A: 衣服   B: 件   C: 做   D: 了   E: 妈妈   F: 给   G: 新   H: 我

745. When I called him, he was eating.
    A: 在   B: 打电话   C: 时候   D: 他   E: 给   F: 吃饭   G: 他   H: 的   I: 我

746. We know it's impossible.
    A: 这   B: 的   C: 是   D: 不   E: 我们   F: 知道   G: 可能

747. No one knows why she doesn't like me.
    A: 没有   B: 为什么   C: 知道   D: 她   E: 我   F: 不   G: 人   H: 喜欢

748. Do you know whose is this?
    A: 吗   B: 的   C: 是   D: 这   E: 你   F: 谁   G: 知道

749. When did it start to rain?
A: 下雨   B: 什么   C: 开始   D: 时候   E: 的

750. He'll tell you.
A: 你   B: 会   C: 的   D: 他   E: 告诉

751. Please tell me where the railway station is.
A: 在   B: 哪儿   C: 我   D: 火车站   E: 请   F: 告诉

752. You'll miss me when I'm gone?
A: 你   B: 我   C: 了   D: 走   E: 想   F: 会   G: 我   H: 吗

753. What do you want me to do?
A: 让   B: 想   C: 你   D: 什么   E: 我   F: 做

754. Do you have any clothes to wash?
A: 衣服   B: 有   C: 你   D: 吗   E: 要   F: 洗   G: 的

755. We'll start as soon as she arrives
A: 我们   B: 一   C: 到   D: 开始   E: 她   F: 就

756. I have a job for you.
A: 有   B: 你   C: 给   D: 工作   E: 我

757. I know she's sleeping.
A: 在   B: 我   C: 知道   D: 她   E: 睡觉

HSK 2 GRAMMAR WORKBOOK

758. I think it's going to be hot today.
   A: 我   B: 很   C: 会   D: 今天   E: 热   F: 觉得

759. Where can I buy it?
   A: 买   B: 到   C: 可以   D: 我   E: 在   F: 哪儿

760. Are you looking for anything?
   A: 找   B: 吗   C: 你   D: 什么   E: 在

761. So it's not hot at all.
   A: 一点儿   B: 所以   C: 热   D: 不   E: 也

762. Why didn't she come yesterday?
   A: 为什么   B: 来   C: 昨天   D: 没   E: 她

763. Is this your book?
   A: 书   B: 您   C: 是   D: 吗   E: 的   F: 这

764. We don't have much time.
   A: 多   B: 我们   C: 没有   D: 太   E: 时间

765. Let's go and play with him.
   A: 找   B: 吧   C: 去   D: 玩儿   E: 我们   F: 他

766. I think he is right.
   A: 对   B: 我   C: 的   D: 觉得   E: 是   F: 他

767. Let's go to bed.

　　A: 去　B: 吧　C: 让　D: 我们　E: 睡觉

768. You can go.

　　A: 去　B: 可以　C: 了　D: 你

769. Who's in this room?

　　A: 房间　B: 里　C: 谁　D: 这个　E: 在

770. I'm waiting for her to talk

　　A: 等　B: 说话　C: 她　D: 在　E: 我

771. He may come today.

　　A: 可能　B: 他　C: 来　D: 今天

772. What did you eat this morning?

　　A: 你　B: 吃　C: 早上　D: 了　E: 今天　F: 什么

773. Do you like school?

　　A: 上学　B: 吗　C: 喜欢　D: 你

774. Are you leaving?

　　A: 要　B: 你　C: 走　D: 了　E: 吗

775. You did better than me.

　　A: 做　B: 你　C: 的　D: 好　E: 我　F: 比

776. How do you know?
   A: 怎么   B: 的   C: 知道   D: 你

777. Her father won't come because he is too busy
   A: 爸爸   B: 太   C: 忙   D: 来   E: 他   F: 不   G: 的   H: 因为   I: 她

778. It is impossible for him to come.
   A: 来   B: 可能   C: 不   D: 他

779. I don't know what you're talking about.
   A: 在   B: 什么   C: 你   D: 懂   E: 我   F: 说   G: 不

780. We all have problems.
   A: 都   B: 问题   C: 我们   D: 有

781. I think I can.
   A: 可以   B: 我   C: 想   D: 我

782. He said he didn't have time.
   A: 没有   B: 他   C: 他   D: 说   E: 时间

783. Your daughter will tell me.
   A: 你   B: 我   C: 会   D: 告诉   E: 女儿

784. I saw him running.
   A: 我   B: 跑步   C: 他   D: 看见   E: 在

785. We won't play basketball tomorrow.
   A: 我们 B: 明天 C: 不 D: 打篮球

786. He is in good health.
   A: 身体 B: 很 C: 好 D: 的 E: 他

787. Let's go play football.
   A: 吧 B: 踢足球 C: 去 D: 我们

788. She doesn't know what?
   A: 知道 B: 什么 C: 不 D: 她

789. I'm sorry I don't have a pencil to write.
   A: 铅笔 B: 没有 C: 写 D: 我 E: 可以 F: 对不起

790. He came to my room.
   A: 来到 B: 他 C: 的 D: 我 E: 房间

791. He is new here.
   A: 的 B: 他 C: 是 D: 新 E: 来

792. Time does not wait for people.
   A: 人 B: 等 C: 时间 D: 不

793. What's wrong with what we're doing
   A: 有 B: 什么 C: 做 D: 问题 E: 的 F: 吗 G: 我们

794. She doesn't like running.

   A: 不 B: 跑步 C: 喜欢 D: 她

795. He is very busy at work.

   A: 忙 B: 很 C: 工作 D: 他

796. Please let us know.

   A: 请 B: 知道 C: 我们 D: 让

797. I like playing football the most.

   A: 喜欢 B: 踢足球 C: 我 D: 最

798. I don't know what I'm doing.

   A: 我 B: 在 C: 什么 D: 做 E: 知道 F: 我 G: 不

799. He is much taller than you.

   A: 他 B: 多 C: 你 D: 高 E: 比 F: 得

800. That's my fault.

   A: 的 B: 是 C: 那 D: 我 E: 错

801. Can I go?

   A: 吗 B: 我 C: 去 D: 可以

802. You're tired, so am I

   A: 我 B: 累 C: 了 D: 累 E: 你 F: 了 G: 也

803. I didn't know you were sleeping.
A: 我 B: 睡觉 C: 在 D: 你 E: 知道 F: 不

804. She is my wife.
A: 是 B: 我 C: 她 D: 妻子

805. You like singing, don't you?
A: 唱歌 B: 你 C: 是 D: 吗 E: 喜欢

806. How many people will know us.
A: 会 B: 有 C: 我们 D: 多少 E: 人 F: 认识

807. Would you like some noodles?
A: 吃 B: 想 C: 你 D: 面条 E: 吗

808. This is my wife.
A: 这 B: 的 C: 妻子 D: 我 E: 是

809. We've arrived.
A: 已经 B: 我们 C: 了 D: 到

810. Don't you know?
A: 你 B: 吗 C: 不 D: 知道

811. I might say yes.
A: 可能 B: 会 C: 我 D: 的 E: 是 F: 说

812. I don't like coffee.

　　A: 我　B: 不　C: 咖啡　D: 喜欢

813. I love you very much.

　　A: 爱　B: 非常　C: 我　D: 你

814. I don't have much time.

　　A: 我　B: 没　C: 了　D: 多少　E: 时间

815. Do you know what that means?

　　A: 吗　B: 你　C: 什么　D: 意思　E: 知道　F: 是　G: 这

816. I'm ready.

　　A: 好　B: 我　C: 准备　D: 了

817. He didn't know what to say.

　　A: 说　B: 他　C: 好　D: 不　E: 什么　F: 知道

818. Because I speak Chinese.

　　A: 说　B: 我　C: 因为　D: 汉语

819. Everyone likes her.

　　A: 喜欢　B: 她　C: 大家　D: 都

820. Would you please wake me up tomorrow morning?

　　A: 请　B: 好　C: 我　D: 吗　E: 叫　F: 明天　G: 早上　H: 起床

821. The book I bought last night has arrived.

   A: 我 B: 的 C: 到 D: 书 E: 买 F: 昨天晚上 G: 了

822. You're right. I'm wrong

   A: 了 B: 错 C: 你 D: 我 E: 说得对

823. Do you have time in the morning?

   A: 吗 B: 上午 C: 时间 D: 你 E: 有

824. She fell in love with her friend's brother.

   A: 上 B: 的 C: 朋友 D: 弟弟 E: 她 F: 爱 G: 她 H: 了

825. She's not busy, is she?

   A: 不 B: 她 C: 忙 D: 对 E: 吗

826. You can go.

   A: 走 B: 了 C: 你 D: 可以

827. Are you listening to me?

   A: 在 B: 您 C: 吗 D: 我 E: 听 F: 说

828. I have class tomorrow.

   A: 明天 B: 有 C: 我 D: 课

829. I don't know now.

   A: 不 B: 现在 C: 知道 D: 我

HSK 2 GRAMMAR WORKBOOK 101

830. Can I go now?

    A: 能   B: 吗   C: 了   D: 我   E: 走   F: 现在

831. I want to dance with you.

    A: 跳舞   B: 你   C: 和   D: 我   E: 想

832. I'll buy you a new one.

    A: 新   B: 买   C: 给   D: 你   E: 的   F: 我   G: 个

833. I don't know what he means.

    A: 我   B: 不   C: 他   D: 意思   E: 的   F: 懂

834. I knew you would come.

    A: 会   B: 知道   C: 就   D: 来   E: 你   F: 我

835. Won't you have some tea with me?

    A: 吗   B: 我   C: 茶   D: 喝   E: 不   F: 点   G: 你   H: 一起   I: 和

836. You can take a taxi.

    A: 你   B: 出租车   C: 坐   D: 可以

837. What day was today last year?

    A: 去年   B: 的   C: 几   D: 星期   E: 今天   F: 是

838. Do you know who wrote this?

    A: 的   B: 吗   C: 这   D: 谁   E: 字   F: 你   G: 是   H: 知道

839. Do you know where I live?

   A: 我   B: 知道   C: 哪儿   D: 吗   E: 住   F: 你

840. It's all your fault.

   A: 错   B: 都   C: 是   D: 你   E: 的

841. I know where you live.

   A: 哪儿   B: 知道   C: 你   D: 住   E: 我

842. I'll give you the money tomorrow.

   A: 给   B: 我   C: 钱   D: 明天   E: 把   F: 你

843. Everyone says I'm wrong.

   A: 错   B: 的   C: 我   D: 说   E: 大家   F: 是   G: 都

844. I live too far away.

   A: 得   B: 我   C: 太   D: 了   E: 远   F: 住

845. I'm not tired now.

   A: 不   B: 累   C: 我   D: 现在

846. I want to know who will go with us.

   A: 谁   B: 和   C: 知道   D: 会   E: 一起   F: 去   G: 想   H: 我们   I: 我

847. How does she talk to people in China?

   A: 人   B: 说话   C: 中国   D: 她   E: 跟   F: 怎么

HSK 2 GRAMMAR WORKBOOK

848. Is this your book?
   A: 的   B: 你   C: 吗   D: 是   E: 书   F: 这

849. I saw her enter the room.
   A: 了   B: 我   C: 进   D: 看见   E: 她   F: 房间

850. It's going to rain tonight.
   A: 下雨   B: 晚上   C: 会   D: 今天

851. Do you like sports?
   A: 你   B: 运动   C: 吗   D: 喜欢

852. Let me go to the shop.
   A: 去   B: 让   C: 商店   D: 我   E: 吧

853. What do you want to learn?
   A: 想   B: 学习   C: 什么   D: 您

854. I'm going to work.
   A: 去   B: 我   C: 准备   D: 上班

855. He swims better than me.
   A: 我   B: 游泳   C: 他   D: 比   E: 好

856. I'd like some coffee thank you.
   A: 我   B: 咖啡   C: 谢谢   D: 要

857. Is this your pencil?
   A: 是 B: 这 C: 你 D: 的 E: 吗 F: 铅笔

858. You don't know who I am.
   A: 您 B: 知道 C: 我 D: 谁 E: 不 F: 是

859. I asked him what his name was.
   A: 名字 B: 他 C: 什么 D: 我 E: 叫 F: 问

860. I had noodles at noon.
   A: 我 B: 面条 C: 中午 D: 吃

861. The person entering the shop is my sister.
   A: 的 B: 进 C: 妹妹 D: 人 E: 商店 F: 是 G: 我

862. I feel very hot.
   A: 热 B: 觉得 C: 我 D: 很

863. She is working now.
   A: 现在 B: 工作 C: 她 D: 正在

864. You're busy right now.
   A: 吧 B: 忙 C: 你 D: 很 E: 现在

865. This is our room.
   A: 是 B: 的 C: 我们 D: 房间 E: 这

HSK 2 GRAMMAR WORKBOOK

866. Your father is waiting for you.
   A: 你 B: 在 C: 呢 D: 你 E: 等 F: 爸爸

867. I don't know where she lives.
   A: 住 B: 在 C: 知道 D: 哪儿 E: 她 F: 我 G: 不

868. What do you think of him?
   A: 他 B: 你 C: 觉得 D: 怎么样

869. Now I like it, too.
   A: 现在 B: 我 C: 喜欢 D: 也

870. I'm busy now.
   A: 着 B: 我 C: 忙 D: 现在 E: 呢

871. Are you busy with your work?
   A: 你 B: 工作 C: 忙 D: 不 E: 忙

872. Please let me know what you want.
   A: 让 B: 想要 C: 什么 D: 你 E: 知道 F: 请 G: 我

873. I like your room.
   A: 喜欢 B: 你 C: 我 D: 房间 E: 的

874. You're tired, are you?
   A: 了 B: 吧 C: 累 D: 你 E: 对

875. We can all go together.

   A: 我们 B: 一起 C: 去 D: 可以

876. Is he going swimming tomorrow?

   A: 游泳 B: 明天 C: 要 D: 吗 E: 他 F: 去

877. We're ready.

   A: 我们 B: 准备 C: 已经 D: 好 E: 了

878. Would you like some more tea?

   A: 再 B: 来 C: 您 D: 点 E: 茶 F: 想 G: 吗

879. Where did you come from?

   A: 的 B: 您 C: 来 D: 哪儿 E: 从

880. I hope he will come tomorrow.

   A: 明天 B: 希望 C: 来 D: 他 E: 会 F: 吧

881. Yes, what do you do?

   A: 工作 B: 什么 C: 对 D: 做 E: 的 F: 了 G: 你

882. Don't talk in the classroom.

   A: 教室 B: 说话 C: 别 D: 里 E: 在

883. I know his name.

   A: 他 B: 知道 C: 的 D: 我 E: 名字

884. I love my wife.
    A: 我   B: 爱   C: 的   D: 我   E: 妻子

885. Did you eat in the classroom
    A: 在   B: 吃   C: 了   D: 您   E: 教室   F: 里   G: 吗

886. Why don't you do it.
    A: 为什么   B: 不   C: 做   D: 你

887. He said he was too busy.
    A: 说   B: 他   C: 太   D: 忙   E: 他   F: 了

888. He will be very busy this week.
    A: 他   B: 忙   C: 星期   D: 这   E: 很   F: 会

889. It's all the cat's fault.
    A: 是   B: 都   C: 猫   D: 的   E: 错

890. Do you have a cell phone?
    A: 您   B: 有   C: 吗   D: 手机

891. We don't know what to do.
    A: 什么   B: 知道   C: 我们   D: 做   E: 不   F: 要

892. I'll ask him tomorrow.
    A: 我   B: 明天   C: 去   D: 问   E: 他

893. What else can I do?

　　A: 什么　B: 能　C: 呢　D: 我　E: 做　F: 还

894. I'll introduce you to my friend.

　　A: 的　B: 我　C: 朋友　D: 介绍　E: 我　F: 给　G: 介绍　H: 你

895. I'm not ready yet.

　　A: 没有　B: 还　C: 我　D: 好　E: 准备

896. I knew you were coming.

　　A: 你　B: 会　C: 来　D: 我　E: 知道　F: 的

897. Ask him the way to the railway station.

　　A: 他　B: 的　C: 火车站　D: 问　E: 路　F: 去

898. I have a question.

　　A: 个　B: 有　C: 我　D: 问题

899. We are very busy now.

　　A: 我们　B: 现在　C: 忙　D: 非常

900. I didn't tell you anything.

　　A: 没有　B: 也　C: 告诉　D: 什么　E: 我　F: 你

901. We can play or sing.

　　A: 也　B: 玩儿　C: 可以　D: 可以　E: 唱歌　F: 我们

HSK 2 GRAMMAR WORKBOOK 109

902. No one in that family has got up yet
    A: 还 B: 家人 C: 那 D: 没 E: 起床

903. I didn't know you were looking at something.
    A: 看 B: 你 C: 不 D: 东西 E: 我 F: 知道 G: 在

904. I like the color, too.
    A: 也 B: 这个 C: 喜欢 D: 颜色 E: 我

905. How many fish did you eat?
    A: 你 B: 鱼 C: 吃 D: 多少 E: 了

906. He asked me what I had bought.
    A: 他 B: 我 C: 问 D: 买 E: 了 F: 什么 G: 些

907. All the students laughed.
    A: 都 B: 了 C: 笑 D: 学生

908. We'll be busy.
    A: 忙 B: 很 C: 会 D: 我们

909. I know too much.
    A: 太 B: 的 C: 我 D: 了 E: 多 F: 知道

910. Don't ask me what this is.
    A: 我 B: 别 C: 东西 D: 是 E: 什么 F: 问 G: 这

911. He will not be happy.
    A: 不会 B: 的 C: 他 D: 高兴

912. Are you busy today?
    A: 忙 B: 今天 C: 吗 D: 你

913. I'm listening to her sing.
    A: 唱歌 B: 她 C: 我 D: 听 E: 正在

914. What are you waiting for?
    A: 什么 B: 等 C: 还 D: 你 E: 呢

915. Dad, do you like noodles?
    A: 吗 B: 你 C: 爸爸 D: 喜欢 E: 面条

916. What are you laughing at?
    A: 什么 B: 呢 C: 笑 D: 在

917. I left the door open.
    A: 门 B: 让 C: 着 D: 开 E: 我

918. Can you swim?
    A: 会 B: 你 C: 吗 D: 游泳

919. Can you wait a minute?
    A: 能 B: 你 C: 吗 D: 等 E: 一下

HSK 2 GRAMMAR WORKBOOK 111

920. We like to sing together.
    A: 喜欢 B: 我们 C: 唱歌 D: 一起

921. What did you give him?
    A: 他 B: 了 C: 给 D: 你 E: 什么

922. There's nothing wrong with that.
    A: 没有 B: 什么 C: 问题 D: 都

923. Are you busy tomorrow afternoon?
    A: 吗 B: 明天 C: 你 D: 下午 E: 忙

924. She doesn't like rice and noodles.
    A: 面条 B: 米饭 C: 喜欢 D: 她 E: 和 F: 不

925. Will you go play, boy?
    A: 孩子 B: 你 C: 去 D: 玩儿 E: 吗 F: 好

926. When does the film start?
    A: 开始 B: 电影 C: 什么 D: 时候

927. Which one is your book?
    A: 您 B: 书 C: 的 D: 本 E: 哪 F: 是

928. Then what will you give me.
    A: 什么 B: 那 C: 我 D: 给 E: 会 F: 你

929. I hope I'll see her again.
    A: 能 B: 她 C: 再 D: 我 E: 希望 F: 看见

930. Whose is this, do you know?
    A: 吗 B: 是 C: 你 D: 知道 E: 谁 F: 这 G: 的

931. She'll be a good wife.
    A: 好 B: 的 C: 妻子 D: 是 E: 会 F: 她 G: 个

932. She asked me how to cook the fish.
    A: 做 B: 鱼 C: 怎么 D: 问 E: 她 F: 我

933. What did you eat tonight?
    A: 晚上 B: 今天 C: 吃 D: 你 E: 什么 F: 了

934. Prepare for tomorrow's exam.
    A: 考试 B: 准备 C: 的 D: 明天

935. Would you like something to drink?
    A: 想 B: 您 C: 什么 D: 点 E: 吗 F: 喝

936. You're wrong if you don't listen to him.
    A: 了 B: 他 C: 的 D: 听 E: 那 F: 就 G: 你 H: 错 I: 不

937. He doesn't know anything.
    A: 都 B: 不 C: 什么 D: 知道 E: 他

HSK 2 GRAMMAR WORKBOOK   113

938. Are you kidding
    A: 说 B: 是 C: 的 D: 玩儿 E: 你 F: 着 G: 吧

939. Please wear something.
    A: 东西 B: 请 C: 穿 D: 点

940. I think it's too big.
    A: 太 B: 我 C: 大 D: 了 E: 觉得

941. I want to buy watermelon.
    A: 西瓜 B: 买 C: 我 D: 想

942. I ate too much.
    A: 多 B: 得 C: 我 D: 了 E: 吃 F: 太

943. This is what I read in the newspaper.
    A: 这 B: 看 C: 的 D: 是 E: 我 F: 在 G: 报纸

944. No one will know.
    A: 会 B: 人 C: 没有 D: 知道

945. We'll come tomorrow.
    A: 明天 B: 再 C: 我们 D: 来

946. Let's go swimming together in the afternoon.
    A: 去 B: 下午 C: 游泳 D: 吧 E: 一起

947. I have something for you.

   A: 我   B: 东西   C: 要   D: 给   E: 你   F: 有

948. Why are there no taxis at the railway station today?

   A: 火车站   B: 为什么   C: 今天   D: 出租车   E: 没有

949. I like Chinese food very much.

   A: 中国   B: 菜   C: 我   D: 非常   E: 喜欢

950. Do you know what you're doing?

   A: 知道   B: 做   C: 你   D: 什么   E: 在   F: 吗   G: 你

951. Everyone knows his name.

   A: 他   B: 都   C: 知道   D: 每个   E: 名字   F: 的   G: 人

952. Don't call me again.

   A: 给   B: 再   C: 别   D: 我   E: 打电话

953. Don't play any more.

   A: 玩儿   B: 别   C: 再   D: 了

954. I'll call you tomorrow.

   A: 你   B: 打电话   C: 明天   D: 我   E: 给

955. Don't tell him I'm here.

   A: 在   B: 他   C: 告诉   D: 别   E: 我   F: 这儿

956. I don't like noodles.
   A: 面条   B: 我   C: 喜欢   D: 不   E: 吃

957. If you have anything you don't understand, ask
   A: 不   B: 就   C: 的   D: 吧   E: 明白   F: 问   G: 如果   H: 什么   I: 你   J: 有

958. I like dogs, my sister likes cats.
   A: 喜欢   B: 妹妹   C: 我   D: 狗   E: 猫   F: 我   G: 喜欢

959. My father is very busy.
   A: 很   B: 我   C: 忙   D: 爸爸

960. Now let's get to work.
   A: 开始   B: 让   C: 工作   D: 现在   E: 我们

961. She asked how that was possible.
   A: 问   B: 她   C: 怎么   D: 可能   E: 这

962. Let's go to the cinema, shall we?
   A: 电影   B: 去   C: 看   D: 让   E: 我们   F: 吗   G: 好

963. I'm happy to be with you
   A: 一起   B: 我   C: 很   D: 在   E: 高兴   F: 和   G: 你

964. Let's go to work.
   A: 工作   B: 吧   C: 大家   D: 去

965. We knew it from the start.
   A: 开始   B: 我们   C: 知道   D: 就   E: 一

966. I'm tired and I want to go to bed.
   A: 想   B: 很   C: 累   D: 睡觉   E: 我   F: 去   G: 我

967. What are you busy with.
   A: 什么   B: 你   C: 忙   D: 在

968. Can I still come?
   A: 我   B: 来   C: 可以   D: 还   E: 吗

969. Your daughter is very tall.
   A: 高   B: 女儿   C: 你   D: 的   E: 很

970. She is playing basketball there.
   A: 正在   B: 打篮球   C: 那儿   D: 她

971. Yes, I know.
   A: 是   B: 我   C: 知道   D: 的

972. I hope your brother is better.
   A: 我   B: 点   C: 了   D: 好   E: 弟弟   F: 希望   G: 你

973. He said we'd have a rest.
   A: 一下   B: 休息   C: 说   D: 他   E: 我们

974. Do you have any questions?

A: 问题 B: 吗 C: 有 D: 你

975. What are you laughing at?

A: 什么 B: 笑 C: 你 D: 呢 E: 在

976. I think you're busy.

A: 忙 B: 你 C: 我 D: 很 E: 想

977. I'm glad to meet you, too.

A: 也 B: 很 C: 认识 D: 你 E: 高兴 F: 我

978. He loves to learn and sports.

A: 爱 B: 也 C: 运动 D: 他 E: 学习 F: 爱

979. What sports do you like best?

A: 运动 B: 什么 C: 最 D: 喜欢 E: 你

980. Can I talk to the teacher?

A: 能 B: 说话 C: 老师 D: 和 E: 吗 F: 我

981. What is everyone talking about?

A: 在 B: 说 C: 什么 D: 呢 E: 大家

982. Do you know who wrote this?

A: 字 B: 你 C: 的 D: 知道 E: 写 F: 是 G: 谁 H: 这 I: 吗

983. It's impossible.
   A: 得到   B: 做   C: 不   D: 可能

984. Has he left?
   A: 已经   B: 走   C: 吗   D: 他   E: 了

985. This gave me new hope.
   A: 给   B: 我   C: 新   D: 的   E: 了   F: 这   G: 希望

986. Why are you running?
   A: 你   B: 在   C: 为什么   D: 跑步

987. I want to know, too.
   A: 知道   B: 我   C: 想   D: 也

988. What are you looking for.
   A: 你   B: 在   C: 找   D: 什么

989. Who gave you this?
   A: 给   B: 的   C: 这个   D: 你   E: 谁

990. No one will listen any more.
   A: 再   B: 会   C: 没有   D: 人   E: 听   F: 了

991. We don't know anyone.
   A: 认识   B: 不   C: 谁   D: 也   E: 我们

992. What about your sister?
    A: 呢   B: 你   C: 姐姐   D: 那

993. It's my fault.
    A: 这   B: 错   C: 的   D: 我   E: 是

994. Do you know what I'm doing?
    A: 做   B: 在   C: 知道   D: 我   E: 吗   F: 你   G: 什么

995. Everyone likes him.
    A: 大家   B: 都   C: 他   D: 喜欢

996. You will play football tomorrow
    A: 你   B: 明天   C: 踢足球   D: 要

997. The weather may be fine tomorrow.
    A: 明天   B: 可能   C: 好   D: 很   E: 天气

998. You can eat what you like.
    A: 吃   B: 东西   C: 你   D: 喜欢   E: 的   F: 可以   G: 你

999. He told me everything.
    A: 都   B: 我   C: 告诉   D: 了   E: 他

1000. I know your name.
    A: 知道   B: 名字   C: 我   D: 你   E: 的

1001. Which course do you like best?

A: 你 B: 课 C: 最 D: 门 E: 哪 F: 喜欢

1002. Everybody's ready.

A: 都 B: 好 C: 了 D: 大家 E: 准备

1003. Can you dance?

A: 吗 B: 你 C: 跳舞 D: 会

1004. He doesn't like fish.

A: 不 B: 喜欢 C: 吃 D: 鱼 E: 他

1005. You know everything, don't you?

A: 吗 B: 都 C: 对 D: 你 E: 知道 F: 什么

1006. He can't be ill.

A: 可能 B: 他 C: 了 D: 不 E: 生病

1007. Her books sell well.

A: 很 B: 卖 C: 好 D: 书 E: 她 F: 得 G: 的

1008. How do we know that?

A: 知道 B: 呢 C: 的 D: 怎么 E: 我们 F: 是

1009. I want to know where she has gone.

A: 我 B: 她 C: 了 D: 去 E: 想 F: 哪儿 G: 知道

1010. When did he start playing football?

　　A: 他　B: 是　C: 什么　D: 的　E: 开始　F: 踢足球　G: 时候

1011. I work in the evening.

　　A: 工作　B: 晚上　C: 在　D: 我

1012. When can I go to see it?

　　A: 去　B: 可以　C: 看　D: 时候　E: 我　F: 什么

1013. You're driving too fast.

　　A: 快　B: 了　C: 太　D: 开　E: 得　F: 你

1014. Can you tell me why you like her?

　　A: 喜欢　B: 告诉　C: 能　D: 吗　E: 你　F: 为什么　G: 我　H: 她　I: 你

1015. Well, you can go if you want

　　A: 吧　B: 好　C: 要　D: 走　E: 走　F: 吧　G: 你　H: 就

1016. She hopes to have a child.

　　A: 希望　B: 孩子　C: 个　D: 有　E: 她

1017. Thank you for calling me.

　　A: 谢谢　B: 给　C: 我　D: 打电话　E: 你

1018. Are you busy now?

　　A: 忙　B: 现在　C: 您　D: 吗

1019. She sat and sang.

A: 她 B: 唱歌 C: 着 D: 坐

1020. Why don't you play basketball at school?

A: 学校 B: 不 C: 你 D: 为什么 E: 打篮球 F: 在

1021. I don't know what to wear.

A: 要 B: 我 C: 不 D: 知道 E: 穿 F: 什么

1022. We're looking for him.

A: 他 B: 找 C: 在 D: 我们

1023. What's wrong with that?

A: 错 B: 什么 C: 有 D: 这

1024. Okay, I'm leaving.

A: 我 B: 了 C: 走 D: 好 E: 要 F: 了

1025. My brother is a teacher.

A: 老师 B: 哥哥 C: 是 D: 的 E: 我

1026. Mother prepared something delicious for me.

A: 好吃 B: 的 C: 我 D: 妈妈 E: 东西 F: 了 G: 给 H: 准备

1027. How far do you have to go?

A: 走 B: 要 C: 你 D: 远 E: 多

1028. When you tell her....

A: 的 B: 告诉 C: 时候 D: 她 E: 你

1029. Do you know who is he?

A: 他 B: 谁 C: 吗 D: 是 E: 你 F: 知道

1030. Go see the doctor.

A: 吧 B: 看 C: 去 D: 医生

1031. Don't ask me anything.

A: 什么 B: 我 C: 别 D: 都 E: 问

1032. I know what you're doing.

A: 在 B: 做 C: 知道 D: 什么 E: 我 F: 你

1033. It makes me very happy.

A: 我 B: 让 C: 高兴 D: 这 E: 很

1034. Would you like something to drink?

A: 要 B: 什么 C: 吗 D: 喝 E: 你 F: 点

1035. I know who she is.

A: 我 B: 知道 C: 谁 D: 她 E: 是

1036. Please give me some water.

A: 水 B: 给 C: 我 D: 请 E: 一点儿

1037. Please give me some water.
   A: 给 B: 一些 C: 水 D: 我 E: 请

1038. I was very busy yesterday.
   A: 我 B: 很 C: 忙 D: 昨天

1039. We're going to dance today.
   A: 要 B: 今天 C: 我们 D: 了 E: 跳舞

1040. Why did you call me?
   A: 给 B: 打电话 C: 我 D: 你 E: 为什么

1041. My room is very small.
   A: 小 B: 房间 C: 的 D: 非常 E: 我

1042. Is that our problem?
   A: 吗 B: 我们 C: 的 D: 问题 E: 是 F: 那

1043. What are you looking for?
   A: 找 B: 您 C: 在 D: 什么

1044. How is that possible?
   A: 这 B: 可能 C: 呢 D: 怎么

1045. When you want to work....
   A: 要 B: 的 C: 工作 D: 时候

1046. He asked my mother.

    A: 问   B: 了   C: 妈妈   D: 他   E: 我

1047. What's wrong with that?

    A: 什么   B: 有   C: 对   D: 吗   E: 不

1048. The chair is far from the door.

    A: 很   B: 门   C: 椅子   D: 远   E: 离

1049. We began to get tired.

    A: 累   B: 了   C: 我们   D: 开始

1050. He asked me why was I laughing.

    A: 为什么   B: 在   C: 问   D: 笑   E: 我   F: 他

1051. You can read your favorite books.

    A: 喜欢   B: 你   C: 可以   D: 的   E: 你   F: 书   G: 读

1052. What time does the movie start?

    A: 时间   B: 电影   C: 什么   D: 开始

1053. Today is my sister's birthday.

    A: 生日   B: 今天   C: 我   D: 的   E: 是   F: 姐姐

1054. What are you going to do tomorrow?

    A: 要   B: 明天   C: 什么   D: 做   E: 你

1055. Please tell me your question.
A: 的   B: 你   C: 告诉   D: 问题   E: 我   F: 请

1056. I know how old you are.
A: 了   B: 多   C: 大   D: 知道   E: 我   F: 你

1057. I very much hope you will come again.
A: 再   B: 希望   C: 来   D: 会   E: 我   F: 很   G: 你

1058. He is a friend of my brother's.
A: 他   B: 是   C: 的   D: 哥哥   E: 我   F: 朋友

1059. I want to go with you.
A: 一起   B: 我   C: 去   D: 你   E: 想   F: 和

1060. The cat is drinking your milk.
A: 猫   B: 你   C: 喝   D: 在   E: 牛奶   F: 的

1061. I think he is very happy.
A: 高兴   B: 他   C: 觉得   D: 很   E: 我

1062. She knows nothing.
A: 不   B: 知道   C: 都   D: 她   E: 什么

1063. I'm waiting for my mother.
A: 妈妈   B: 着   C: 我   D: 我   E: 等

1064. What to eat tonight.
A: 吃   B: 什么   C: 晚上   D: 今天

HSK 2 GRAMMAR WORKBOOK

1065. Don't start without me
    A: 在 B: 我 C: 开始 D: 别 E: 就 F: 不

1066. How much do you want?
    A: 钱 B: 你 C: 多少 D: 要

1067. Ask him his name.
    A: 问 B: 名字 C: 的 D: 一下 E: 他 F: 他

1068. I like you, too.
    A: 喜欢 B: 也 C: 你 D: 我

1069. The child has no friends.
    A: 孩子 B: 那 C: 没有 D: 朋友 E: 什么

1070. This means zero.
    A: 意思 B: 是 C: 这 D: 的 E: 零

1071. He's here to find a job.
    A: 找 B: 是 C: 工作 D: 他 E: 来 F: 的

1072. Do you have a younger brother?
    A: 你 B: 吗 C: 有 D: 弟弟

1073. He bought new clothes for his daughter.
    A: 衣服 B: 给 C: 了 D: 新 E: 女儿 F: 他 G: 买

1074. Sit wherever you like.

A: 喜欢 B: 就 C: 你 D: 坐 E: 哪儿 F: 坐 G: 哪儿

1075. I like noodles best.

A: 面条 B: 最 C: 我 D: 吃 E: 喜欢

1076. Does he want to play basketball?

A: 要 B: 打篮球 C: 吗 D: 他

1077. I asked him if he was busy.

A: 忙 B: 不 C: 忙 D: 问 E: 我 F: 他

1078. I like my work very much.

A: 我 B: 我 C: 非常 D: 的 E: 喜欢 F: 工作

1079. I don't know what to say.

A: 我 B: 不 C: 说 D: 什么 E: 知道

1080. I'd like to have a rest.

A: 我 B: 休息 C: 想 D: 一下

1081. I'm in very good health.

A: 我 B: 非常 C: 好 D: 身体

1082. I'll call you as soon as I get to the airport.

A: 给 B: 了 C: 机场 D: 打电话 E: 你 F: 我 G: 就 H: 到 I: 一

1083. The computer is new.
　　A: 电脑　B: 的　C: 新　D: 是

1084. I don't read the newspaper very much.
　　A: 报纸　B: 看　C: 不怎么　D: 我

1085. We can't see him when we wait and wait
　　A: 我们　B: 去　C: 看不见　D: 等　E: 他　F: 来　G: 都　H: 等

1086. She bought a newspaper.
　　A: 她　B: 买　C: 了　D: 报纸

1087. Do you know what to say?
　　A: 说　B: 吗　C: 知道　D: 你　E: 怎么

1088. Are you coming tomorrow?
　　A: 来　B: 要　C: 吗　D: 明天　E: 你

1089. She likes her school very much.
　　A: 非常　B: 她　C: 喜欢　D: 的　E: 学校　F: 她

1090. I'll leave when he comes.
　　A: 了　B: 我　C: 等　D: 他　E: 来　F: 走　G: 就

1091. I like fish and rice.
　　A: 喜欢　B: 鱼　C: 和　D: 米饭　E: 吃　F: 我

1092. He is already dressed.

　　A: 他　B: 衣服　C: 了　D: 好　E: 穿　F: 已经

1093. Is this your room?

　　A: 你　B: 是　C: 房间　D: 吗　E: 这　F: 的

1094. I have bought it.

　　A: 买　B: 它　C: 我　D: 已经　E: 了

1095. It's all my fault.

　　A: 都　B: 我　C: 是　D: 的　E: 错

1096. Can I know your name?

　　A: 知道　B: 的　C: 吗　D: 名字　E: 能　F: 你　G: 我

1097. I'm glad you're right.

　　A: 的　B: 对　C: 你　D: 高兴　E: 我　F: 是　G: 很

1098. Tell me what you want me to buy you.

　　A: 你　B: 让　C: 什么　D: 想　E: 给　F: 买　G: 告诉　H: 我　I: 我　J: 你

1099. I like snow so much.

　　A: 喜欢　B: 好　C: 我　D: 雪

1100. You're right.

　　A: 很　B: 得　C: 对　D: 说　E: 你

HSK 2 GRAMMAR WORKBOOK 131

1101. You know what I mean?

A: 知道   B: 意思   C: 吗   D: 我   E: 你   F: 的

1102. Would you like some milk?

A: 吗   B: 牛奶   C: 要   D: 点   E: 来

1103. When will we arrive?

A: 到   B: 什么   C: 我们   D: 时候

1104. Can we go to the movies?

A: 可以   B: 看   C: 电影   D: 去   E: 我们   F: 吗

1105. It may rain in the evening.

A: 会   B: 下雨   C: 晚上   D: 可能

1106. You make me happy.

A: 快乐   B: 我   C: 你   D: 让

1107. He said he was off the subject.

A: 他   B: 说   C: 题   D: 离   E: 了

1108. Can I come again?

A: 吗   B: 还   C: 可以   D: 我   E: 再   F: 来

1109. Can you get up?

A: 能   B: 你   C: 起床   D: 吗

1110. I prepared the lamb.

A: 我   B: 准备   C: 了   D: 羊肉

1111. Let's go play basketball.

A: 去   B: 我们   C: 吧   D: 打篮球

1112. It's impossible.

A: 是   B: 的   C: 不   D: 这   E: 可能

1113. I want to go swimming.

A: 去   B: 我   C: 游泳   D: 想

1114. Can I see your ticket?

A: 的   B: 你   C: 我   D: 可以   E: 一下   F: 票   G: 看   H: 吗

1115. My brother is a teacher.

A: 是   B: 弟弟   C: 老师   D: 我   E: 的

1116. I called him yesterday.

A: 打电话   B: 给   C: 我   D: 他   E: 昨天

1117. I like watermelon very much.

A: 吃   B: 西瓜   C: 喜欢   D: 我   E: 很

1118. I'm playing football now.

A: 正在   B: 我   C: 现在   D: 踢足球

HSK 2 GRAMMAR WORKBOOK 133

1119. How far do we have to go?

A: 走   B: 要   C: 我们   D: 远   E: 多

1120. Why are you still at school?

A: 在   B: 学校   C: 还   D: 为什么   E: 你

1121. I'm glad you like it

A: 高兴   B: 喜欢   C: 就   D: 你   E: 我

1122. I'll go with him.

A: 一起   B: 走   C: 我   D: 和   E: 他

1123. I have no time and no money.

A: 时间   B: 钱   C: 没有   D: 没有   E: 也   F: 我

1124. Would you like some tea?

A: 吗   B: 茶   C: 你   D: 要   E: 喝   F: 点

1125. The chair is close to the door.

A: 椅子   B: 近   C: 离   D: 很   E: 门

1126. She is very good at singing.

A: 她   B: 会   C: 很   D: 唱歌

1127. I like your coffee.

A: 我   B: 你   C: 的   D: 喜欢   E: 咖啡

1128. There's something I want to say to you.

A: 有   B: 要   C: 说   D: 对   E: 你   F: 我   G: 事情   H: 件

1129. She began to sing.

A: 开始   B: 她   C: 唱歌   D: 了

1130. The taxi is coming.

A: 快   B: 了   C: 出租车   D: 来

1131. I don't know what can we do.

A: 能   B: 我   C: 不   D: 什么   E: 我们   F: 知道   G: 做

1132. I can call her.

A: 给   B: 能   C: 我   D: 她   E: 打电话

1133. She didn't go far.

A: 她   B: 远   C: 走   D: 没   E: 多

1134. Does the hotel have a computer?

A: 吗   B: 宾馆   C: 有   D: 电脑

1135. She may come.

A: 会   B: 可能   C: 来   D: 她

1136. I don't know what you're thinking.

A: 不   B: 知道   C: 你   D: 在   E: 什么   F: 想   G: 我

1137. I hope you'll like it.

　　A: 会　B: 希望　C: 你　D: 喜欢

ANSWER

1. 我不知道穿什么好
2. 我在吃面条
3. 我没有带手机
4. 你在笑什么
5. 我们明天什么时候到
6. 你的学校有多远
7. 我还不知道
8. 请告诉我一些事情
9. 你现在可以开始了
10. 你怎么知道那是我最喜欢的
11. 我给她打电话的时候她不在
12. 请给我点水
13. 你今天有什么事情要做吗
14. 您昨天在哪儿
15. 你为什么在这
16. 我希望你去
17. 请问去火车站怎么走
18. 她没有真正的朋友
19. 她没有告诉我她的名字
20. 帮助她是我们的工作
21. 这是你要的吗

22. 你说得太多了
23. 他喜欢唱歌也喜欢跳舞
24. 她是我的姐姐
25. 有茶和咖啡你喜欢什么
26. 我要我们一起做
27. 他很喜欢旅游
28. 我在等公共汽车
29. 我也喜欢跳舞
30. 它正在吃米饭
31. 她要睡觉了
32. 你知道她是谁吗
33. 她也会来吗
34. 您有铅笔吗
35. 我比你漂亮
36. 她很喜欢跳舞
37. 我们坐出租车去吧
38. 因为大家都没有钱了
39. 我想吃面条
40. 今天早上很冷
41. 我不喜欢猫我弟弟也不喜欢
42. 你不可以和我们一起去
43. 因为它太大了
44. 我想和你一起去但是我没有时间

45. 我什么都知道
46. 她**爱**她的孩子
47. 我很**爱**她但是她不**爱**我
48. 再来点茶好**吗**
49. 我知道一些事情
50. 你的**电脑**有什么**问题**
51. 我不明白你的意思
52. 你想知道我看**见**了什么**吗**
53. 我知道她不**爱**他
54. 他要睡**觉**了
55. 我知道她不**爱**它
56. 很有可能再次下雨
57. **这**是你的**颜**色
58. 他想和我**们**一起去看**电**影
59. 我**觉**得你喜**欢**她
60. 昨天吃了**鱼**
61. 可以走了吧
62. 我不知道你什么意思
63. 他比他的弟弟高
64. 我不知道他什么**时**候再来
65. 正在踢足球的那个学生是你的同学**吗**
66. 你看**过**多少次了
67. 你**给**我唱歌
68. 有多少个西瓜

69. 你喜欢跑步吗
70. 他喜欢我我也喜欢他
71. 水果对身体非常好
72. 我早上要去跑步
73. 他想什么时候起床就什么时候起床
74. 请你把门开着好吗
75. 她帮助了他
76. 你知道我是谁
77. 你丈夫叫什么名字
78. 你在找工作吗
79. 到机场有多远
80. 今天早上很热呢
81. 有什么新东西
82. 他坐公共汽车上班
83. 我可以吃点东西吗
84. 你最喜欢什么水果
85. 你能再给我点茶吗
86. 明天打电话给我
87. 你在和谁说话
88. 我到家给你打电话
89. 你咖啡喝得太多了
90. 别说话听我说
91. 你能把门打开吗

92. 你为什么不去

93. 你晚上给我打电话了吗

94. 你的衣服是什么颜色的

95. 他问了我的妈妈

96. 我明白你的意思

97. 你现在想打篮球吗

98. 他是我的哥哥

99. 到我前面去

100. 我会帮你准备好的

101. 他知道我是谁吗

102. 昨天是我的生日

103. 我不知道他什么时候来

104. 他是我弟弟

105. 你的孩子多大了

106. 那我懂你的意思了

107. 你早上吃了什么

108. 您要多少钱

109. 我要去看电影

110. 你喜欢你的新工作吗

111. 为什么你想知道我在想什么

112. 我想认识你姐姐

113. 你愿意一起跳舞吗

114. 这个什么时候准备好

115. 穿上点衣服

116. 我想吃点好吃的
117. 我能看一下您的票吗
118. 去我们学校比去火车站要远
119. 你能游泳吗
120. 是的我也是学生
121. 我们去游泳吧
122. 你认识他哥哥吗
123. 我觉得这要看的吧
124. 你怎么到那儿的
125. 他觉得我爱她
126. 你什么时候上班
127. 他今天开始工作
128. 我不喜欢踢足球
129. 我希望我可以去
130. 他不知道他在说什么
131. 爸爸给我买了本书
132. 虽然我很累但是我已经做了我能做的了
133. 你想对我说什么
134. 我想知道谁来了
135. 谁告诉你的
136. 就别告诉他
137. 没人告诉我在哪里可以找到你
138. 这是什么意思

139. 我从一开始就错了
140. 你怎么做都可以
141. 他妻子是我女儿
142. 到了给我打电话
143. 我去洗一洗
144. 我的意思是
145. 他知道你爱他吗
146. 我们的时间不多
147. 好的我再吃点
148. 今天的报纸我还没有看
149. 你今天要做什么
150. 谁也不知道
151. 这是火车站吗
152. 大家都在等你
153. 您的家在哪
154. 我不懂你的意思
155. 您叫什么名字
156. 我还没准备好
157. 告诉我你要什么
158. 他说可能要下雨
159. 您在做什么菜
160. 我认识她的姐姐
161. 你现在忙吗
162. 我不知道你在说什么

163. 你想去旅游吗

164. 我现在非常忙

165. 她可能在教室里

166. 你爸爸很忙吗

167. 你能来就来

168. 她问了他一个问题

169. 你最好吃点东西

170. 你知道的太多了

171. 你觉得会有什么问题吗

172. 他忙着工作

173. 我想我喝得太多了

174. 我正在学习汉语

175. 您在找什么吗

176. 已经到了吗

177. 他对我很好

178. 我今天不忙

179. 我不知道他的姓

180. 我说了可能要下雨

181. 你来点面条吗

182. 我想买一个便宜一点的

183. 我可以等你

184. 有时间我就来

185. 你觉得哪儿好就去哪儿

186. 我想我要去睡觉了

187. 你身体好吗
188. 她非常喜欢唱歌
189. 请告诉我你的名字
190. 她姐姐比我哥哥大
191. 你笑什么呢
192. 你想去游泳吗
193. 别进我的房间
194. 我知道你不喜欢他
195. 明天可能会下雨
196. 她可能比你高
197. 你怎么还不睡觉
198. 我们开始吃吧
199. 谁也不知道为什么
200. 到火车站有多远
201. 今天我要去看他
202. 我去年认识了他
203. 对不起我错了
204. 她也喜欢吃面条
205. 我很高兴你来了
206. 还在下雨吗
207. 她是个非常好的老师
208. 我认识他但是我不知道他的名字
209. 天气非常好是吧

210. 你知道他的名字吗

211. 你想知道吗

212. 您喜欢去哪儿就去哪儿

213. 他打电话来的时候我正在忙

214. 我知道他忙

215. 有朋友真好

216. 我不知道是什么意思

217. 我不知道你想说什么

218. 你知道她什么时候来吗

219. 你能给我来点茶吗

220. 我很喜欢跳舞

221. 我开始冷了

222. 这是我的妹妹

223. 他不知道我是谁

224. 我进了她的房间

225. 你为什么问我

226. 所以我们都非常忙

227. 我不知道你怎么想

228. 我和我的丈夫都是老师

229. 我不知道我写得对不对

230. 你从昨天开始就忙吗

231. 我想介绍你给他认识

232. 我听不太懂你的意思

233. 你已经到家了吗
234. 你是怎么知道的
235. 你想吃多少就吃多少
236. 没有人在房间里
237. 你喜欢唱歌吗
238. 你知道怎么做吗
239. 零在一前面
240. 因为她是新来的所以她谁都不认识
241. 我们要睡觉了
242. 我的妹妹是老师
243. 那飞机真大
244. 我们一起在学校
245. 我知道你喜欢我
246. 请你让我一下好吗
247. 没有人会找你
248. 你知道我们做了什么吗
249. 你是新来的吗
250. 你的丈夫喜欢这个孩子吗
251. 我知道他住哪儿
252. 你做的菜真好吃
253. 我希望他能来
254. 她晚上做什么
255. 请你告诉我路怎么走好吗
256. 他买了块手表给我

257. 给我点喝的
258. 我知道你为什么高兴
259. 那是谁给你的
260. 我有个哥哥
261. 我不知道他也不知道
262. 我要去饭店
263. 你能告诉我这是什么吗
264. 我想让你准备好
265. 我知道他很忙
266. 他明天会很忙
267. 你是什么意思
268. 我想我是对的
269. 我要做的事情都已经做了
270. 你比我还高
271. 你为什么不知道
272. 你妹妹今天穿的衣服多漂亮啊
273. 你想怎么做就怎么做
274. 对不起我现在很忙
275. 你的时间到了
276. 我也不喜欢她
277. 你做完了吗
278. 她比我高得多
279. 没有人知道她在哪儿
280. 我不知道他叫什么名字

281. 今天很可能会下雨
282. 你喜欢什么运动
283. 你姐姐是学生吗
284. 我们休息一下吧好吗
285. 你有手机吗
286. 上午你有时间吗
287. 请你等一下好吗
288. 谢谢你一起和我跳舞
289. 他长得高吗
290. 我不太懂您的意思
291. 他说话太快了
292. 你想买什么给他
293. 他和我说了要去哪
294. 教室里没有人
295. 那是明天吧
296. 你知道眼睛为什么长在前面吗
297. 我们都非常想你
298. 他可能在教室里
299. 让我们开始吧
300. 我知道我什么都不知道
301. 你准备好开始了吗
302. 我想知道她的名字
303. 我们知道我们在做什么

304. 你不觉得冷吗

305. 你没有时间了

306. 你知道我住哪吗

307. 让我们上饭馆去

308. 在找什么呢

309. 我还在学习

310. 我们说到哪儿了

311. 他已经走了

312. 我想我知道他是谁

313. 我们告诉他什么

314. 你哥哥身体好吗

315. 他姐姐比我哥哥大

316. 你想再喝点咖啡吗

317. 现在你想让我怎么做

318. 我从中国来的

319. 我们正在吃苹果

320. 明天是我生日

321. 我都知道了

322. 我不知道他星期几来

323. 我知道你喜欢咖啡

324. 就快到家了

325. 你可以等一下吗

326. 她和她爸爸打篮球

327. 我身体很好

328. 你爱什么时候去就什么时候去
329. 你在找什么呢
330. 有比没有好
331. 火车站就在旁边
332. 房间里没有人
333. 她给她妈妈打电话
334. 我在房间里睡觉
335. 让我们知道你什么时候到
336. 没有他的帮助我也能做
337. 我在找我的朋友
338. 我非常想去
339. 我不知道我们什么时候可以吃
340. 你什么时候开始工作
341. 给我点东西吃
342. 我的狗比你的小
343. 我要坐出租车去
344. 告诉我您在想什么
345. 好我们开始工作吧
346. 我还喜欢你
347. 妈妈我能去游泳吗
348. 谢谢你给我的帮助
349. 这是个鸡蛋
350. 你今天为什么这么忙

351. 请叫他等一下
352. 你要喝点咖啡吗
353. 大家都认识我
354. 您想吃点什么吗
355. 穿你想穿的
356. 我可能错了
357. 不在她正在上班
358. 你给了我什么
359. 我喝了牛奶
360. 今天是我的生日
361. 他已经来了吗
362. 你还能告诉我什么
363. 你喜欢吃西瓜吗
364. 我们问他叫什么名字
365. 我知道怎么做
366. 我也可以去吗
367. 但是不太多
368. 我要去医院
369. 那我明天再问他
370. 所以他没有去学校
371. 您想喝什么
372. 我不知道为什么你不喜欢她
373. 我们现在要去睡觉
374. 你已经有孩子了吗

375. 你还不睡觉
376. 我知道您也很忙
377. 今天早上你在做什么
378. 你去年住在哪儿
379. 我能喝一杯吗
380. 你懂我的意思
381. 请给我水就好了
382. 你走了我们都会想你的
383. 昨天天气非常好
384. 我要和你说再见了
385. 我想他会来的吧
386. 我正在看报纸
387. 我不知道他是谁
388. 工作的时候工作休息的时候休息
389. 谢谢你的帮助
390. 对不起请问去火车站怎么走
391. 你让我做什么我就做什么
392. 我没有看见它你也没有看见它
393. 我非常想你
394. 你为什么在这里
395. 我已经不爱他了
396. 你喜欢咖啡吗
397. 再找时间吧

398. 你打电话给她了吗
399. 我们什么都知道
400. 你知道她喜欢什么颜色吗
401. 你的房间在哪
402. 谁让她来的
403. 我不知道她是谁
404. 他喜欢面条吗
405. 我昨天来就好了
406. 我不知道要做什么
407. 我知道他叫什么名字
408. 这是谁的椅子
409. 你还想再吃点面条吗
410. 你比她要高
411. 我哪儿也不去
412. 不知道明天天气会怎么样呢
413. 我觉得很快乐
414. 想吃什么就吃什么吧
415. 我能帮助她
416. 我不知道谁要来
417. 我们坐出租车吧
418. 我等着出租车
419. 去工作吧再见
420. 我们还在吃着呢

421. 帮助你是我们的工作
422. 你去我就去
423. 你们为什么都不说话
424. 您今天做了什么
425. 他是我非常好的朋友
426. 让我们坐公共汽车去
427. 他对你说了些什么
428. 咖啡是冷的
429. 你喜欢雪吗
430. 来吧我们一起去
431. 我不喜欢茶也不喜欢咖啡
432. 他等了很长的时间
433. 他不听我说话
434. 我不知道他在哪
435. 我希望你能来和我一起工作
436. 他也学习汉语
437. 是谁的错呢
438. 你正在想什么
439. 好吧我们走吧
440. 他问我快不快乐
441. 他正在做面条
442. 你想做什么就做什么
443. 今天鱼很便宜
444. 请到前面来

445. 您想吃什么
446. 他来了我们就开始
447. 他问你什么
448. 让我们问老师
449. 他会是我妹妹的好丈夫的
450. 我知道你是老师
451. 他下个月会很忙
452. 你的手表在哪儿
453. 他会是个好丈夫的
454. 这要多少钱
455. 去吃点东西吧
456. 你哥哥是谁
457. 你知道他说了什么吗
458. 你什么时候去
459. 喝点咖啡吗
460. 我明天再做
461. 你的妹妹呢
462. 我觉得是你
463. 你一准备好我们就走
464. 我也不喜欢
465. 她不喜欢她的丈夫
466. 我的姐姐有工作
467. 我们要做的工作太多了
468. 我儿子比我高

469. 你能让她打电话给我吗

470. 我可以帮助你吗

471. 你不忙对吧

472. 我也不喜欢他

473. 你什么时候走

474. 我知道他是谁

475. 您最喜欢什么水果

476. 我现在没有时间

477. 我昨天生病了

478. 我觉得我们可以做好朋友

479. 这是个时间问题

480. 他开始找工作了

481. 面条和米饭都很好吃

482. 你喜欢游泳吗

483. 我到火车站了

484. 我不喜欢吃鸡蛋

485. 我就在你后面

486. 你的衣服是什么颜色

487. 我们明天上午开始

488. 你的姓怎么读

489. 你为什么喜欢我

490. 你可以看这书

491. 我不喜欢吃西瓜

492. 不知道他什么时候来
493. 他很可能知道我喜欢他
494. 你可能是对的
495. 有什么问题吗
496. 他可能不高兴
497. 你的手表比我的贵
498. 妈妈说我说话太快
499. 这就是我们想知道的
500. 她告诉我她妈妈买给她了
501. 你也要去吗
502. 你明天就可以休息
503. 我知道那是什么
504. 你和我们一起吃吗
505. 他喜欢看报纸
506. 我觉得他是医生
507. 你爸爸很高
508. 我们的饭店比那家饭店好
509. 我觉得工作很忙
510. 你觉得累吗
511. 没有人能知道
512. 我为什么要给他钱
513. 这是要卖的东西吗
514. 你现在觉得好点了吗

515. 你有时间再做吧
516. 我没有你高
517. 你说得不对
518. 现在你忙吗
519. 您晚上给我打电话了吗
520. 她喜欢好吃的东西
521. 你问题太多了
522. 医生给我开了药
523. 我在等我的朋友
524. 你可以告诉我我错在哪儿吗
525. 她告诉我她认识我的哥哥
526. 明天是她的生日
527. 我是新来的
528. 你想走的时候就走吧
529. 你还可以吃点米饭
530. 没有人知道他的真名字
531. 明天的课我能不来吗
532. 可以便宜点吗
533. 我可以问你个问题吗
534. 我们现在就去医院吧
535. 是你准备好茶的时候了
536. 我爸爸告诉你他去哪儿了
537. 那是我最喜欢的椅子

538. 我明天会很忙
539. 我们不知道他来不来
540. 我知道我做错了
541. 他很会说笑
542. 你已经要走了吗
543. 你想吃什么就吃什么
544. 我知道你还爱我
545. 他可能喜欢他的工作
546. 你知道我的名字吗
547. 我在学校前面等你
548. 我没有休息的时间
549. 我哪也不去
550. 今天早上非常冷
551. 我一点儿都不懂
552. 我在找工作
553. 我不认识她我也不知道她是谁
554. 你是在对我说吗
555. 他让我做我就做了
556. 我姐姐比我哥哥大
557. 他非常喜欢他的学校
558. 我很喜欢旅游
559. 她给了他些热的喝
560. 我也想去北京
561. 他爱她她也爱他

562. 我们的教室非常小

563. 她唱歌非常好

564. 他走得非常慢

565. 但是我没有钱

566. 谢谢你来火车站送我

567. 给我你的手机

568. 我想你也会喜欢的

569. 它的颜色是红的

570. 我很高兴我能帮助你

571. 我是你的妹妹

572. 我要睡觉了

573. 你有孩子吗

574. 这是我的问题

575. 明天很有可能下雨

576. 我有个弟弟

577. 让我看一下你买的东西

578. 我觉得你正在做的是错的

579. 大家都在哪儿

580. 我一到机场就给你打电话

581. 我们都累了

582. 没有人听我说话

583. 你早上什么时候起床

584. 我认为你是对的

585. 你能告诉我怎么去火车站吗

586. 他看了看手表

587. 你能不能不告诉他

588. 我知道你做了什么

589. 我每天早上都去买东西

590. 告诉我什么时候开始

591. 我不知道那是什么

592. 你还认识我吗

593. 电影已经开始了吗

594. 我要他等我

595. 我很喜欢雪

596. 你知道我想听什么

597. 我不喜欢鸡蛋

598. 我想吃点鱼

599. 你喜欢吃鱼吗

600. 您是这里的学生吗

601. 你能给我吗

602. 你能来一下吗

603. 这东西我买得很便宜

604. 我现在很累

605. 她对我说她喜欢你

606. 喂你还在吗

607. 我已经累了

608. 眼睛为什么长在前面
609. 我的狗是白的
610. 七比九少二
611. 你想去打篮球吗
612. 为什么你不休息一下
613. 我希望他会等我
614. 她可能不来了
615. 你有什么问题
616. 这是我最喜欢的
617. 你的眼睛真漂亮
618. 他会告诉我我真正想要什么吗
619. 你跑步了吗
620. 我喜欢和你在一起
621. 你懂我的意思吗
622. 你有铅笔吗
623. 我是你的朋友对吗
624. 我们可以一起走
625. 他可能明天下午来
626. 我问你在想什么
627. 我们是好朋友对吧
628. 我叫你去你为什么不去
629. 他在她的旁边
630. 你想喝点咖啡吗

631. 你怎么会不知道
632. 你的姐姐呢
633. 你能告诉我你住哪儿
634. 我妈妈让我吃点药
635. 我明天上午给你打电话
636. 你要唱歌吗
637. 我们明天要去跳舞
638. 你不准备去是吗
639. 好吧我懂了谢谢你
640. 我明天晚上来
641. 他一开始就不喜欢她
642. 你在上班吗
643. 我知道我错了
644. 卖给我们吧
645. 可能要下雨了
646. 我非常喜欢咖啡
647. 大家都认识她
648. 他说了他也爱我
649. 我希望你会喜欢它
650. 去找工作怎么样
651. 他问老师为什么让他看电影
652. 我不觉得她漂亮
653. 我认识她的妹妹

654. 我的生日就快到了
655. 我很想知道她的名字
656. 现在谁在笑
657. 我可以明天开始
658. 你什么时候开始打篮球的
659. 明天有可能会下雨
660. 我觉得你的工作还可以
661. 她爸爸很高
662. 你为什么不给我打电话
663. 我叫你怎么做你就怎么做
664. 我非常喜欢你
665. 您可以走了
666. 我希望这是对的
667. 为什么你不说话
668. 明天会好的
669. 我不知道他什么时候能来
670. 她在找工作
671. 我吃点面条
672. 我们到的时候正在下雨
673. 您的朋友会想您的
674. 他能读得很好
675. 他还说了什么
676. 我去上汉语课
677. 你能告诉我吗
678. 你也是个儿子

679. 你想知道些什么
680. 请给我打电话
681. 那我们要做什么
682. 我知道你会的
683. 她也学习汉语
684. 我今天早上看了电视
685. 你最喜欢的颜色是什么
686. 请你告诉我机场怎么去
687. 她什么时候到家
688. 你做得很好
689. 我什么都不知道
690. 他没有做错
691. 让我看一下你的票
692. 你正在做什么
693. 鱼和羊肉在一起不好吃
694. 你为什么不听
695. 这是给你的
696. 我想和你一起走
697. 我也不知道
698. 我们休息一下吧
699. 她进了房间
700. 但是我的生日就在明天
701. 我明天会打电话给你
702. 我爱她她也爱我

703. 你有今天的票吗

704. 我现在在机场

705. 我看见她在游泳

706. 我一点儿钱也没有

707. 你要多少个苹果

708. 我们什么时候可以吃饭

709. 我们都非常喜欢你

710. 我们对你知道得不多

711. 现在你要听些什么

712. 我的房间号码是多少

713. 我的家离学校很近

714. 我可以来听你的课吗

715. 你知道他住哪儿吗

716. 她知道你吗

717. 在找东西吗

718. 我不知道你要去哪

719. 你爱去哪儿我们就去哪儿

720. 我汉语老师是男的

721. 我现在不忙

722. 我们一起去学校

723. 我现在很忙

724. 我明天可以打电话给你吗

725. 我累了让我们睡觉吧

726. 你明天什么时候起床
727. 我非常喜欢它
728. 我上完了课很累
729. 你能把它写下来吗
730. 有东西进入我的眼睛
731. 我昨天不忙
732. 你觉得这米饭怎么样
733. 我们去睡觉吧
734. 我觉得你累
735. 没关系我可以等
736. 飞机准备好了
737. 他告诉我她生病了
738. 我可能吃得最多
739. 现在我可以走了吗
740. 给她点时间
741. 你爱吃面条吗
742. 我知道你是对的
743. 但是你有孩子
744. 妈妈给我做了件新衣服
745. 我给他打电话的时候他在吃饭
746. 我们知道这是不可能的
747. 没有人知道为什么她不喜欢我
748. 你知道这是谁的吗

749. 什么时候开始下雨的

750. 他会告诉你的

751. 请告诉我火车站在哪儿

752. 我走了你会想我吗

753. 你想让我做什么

754. 你有要洗的衣服吗

755. 她一到我们就开始

756. 我有工作给你

757. 我知道她在睡觉

758. 我觉得今天会很热

759. 我在哪儿可以买到

760. 你在找什么吗

761. 所以一点儿也不热

762. 她昨天为什么没来

763. 这是您的书吗

764. 我们没有太多时间

765. 我们去找他玩儿吧

766. 我觉得他是对的

767. 让我们去睡觉吧

768. 你可以去了

769. 谁在这个房间里

770. 我在等她说话

771. 他今天可能来
772. 你今天早上吃了什么
773. 你喜欢上学吗
774. 你要走了吗
775. 你做的比我好
776. 你怎么知道的
777. 她的爸爸不来因为他太忙
778. 他不可能来
779. 我不懂你在说什么
780. 我们都有问题
781. 我想我可以
782. 他说他没有时间
783. 你女儿会告诉我
784. 我看见他在跑步
785. 我们明天不打篮球
786. 他的身体很好
787. 我们去踢足球吧
788. 她不知道什么
789. 对不起我没有铅笔可以写
790. 他来到我的房间
791. 他是新来的
792. 时间不等人
793. 我们做的有什么问题吗
794. 她不喜欢跑步

795. 他工作很忙
796. 请让我们知道
797. 我最喜欢踢足球
798. 我不知道我在做什么
799. 他比你高得多
800. 那是我的错
801. 我可以去吗
802. 你累了我也累了
803. 我不知道你在睡觉
804. 她是我妻子
805. 你喜欢唱歌是吗
806. 有多少人会认识我们
807. 你想吃面条吗
808. 这是我的妻子
809. 我们已经到了
810. 你不知道吗
811. 我可能会说是的
812. 我不喜欢咖啡
813. 我非常爱你
814. 我没多少时间了
815. 你知道这是什么意思吗
816. 我准备好了
817. 他不知道说什么好

818. 因为我说汉语
819. 大家都喜欢她
820. 明天早上请叫我起床好吗
821. 我昨天晚上买的书到了
822. 你说得对我错了
823. 你上午有时间吗
824. 她爱上了她朋友的弟弟
825. 她不忙对吗
826. 你可以走了
827. 您在听我说吗
828. 我明天有课
829. 我现在不知道
830. 我现在能走了吗
831. 我想和你跳舞
832. 我给你买个新的
833. 我不懂他的意思
834. 我就知道你会来
835. 你不和我一起喝点茶吗
836. 你可以坐出租车
837. 去年的今天是星期几
838. 你知道这是谁的字吗
839. 你知道我住哪儿吗
840. 都是你的错

841. 我知道你住哪儿
842. 我明天把钱给你
843. 大家都说我是错的
844. 我住得太远了
845. 我现在不累
846. 我想知道谁会和我们一起去
847. 她怎么跟中国人说话
848. 这是你的书吗
849. 我看见她进了房间
850. 今天晚上会下雨
851. 你喜欢运动吗
852. 让我去商店吧
853. 您想学习什么
854. 我准备去上班
855. 他游泳比我好
856. 我要咖啡谢谢
857. 这是你的铅笔吗
858. 您不知道我是谁
859. 我问他叫什么名字
860. 中午我吃面条
861. 进商店的人是我妹妹
862. 我觉得很热
863. 她现在正在工作

864. 你现在很忙吧
865. 这是我们的房间
866. 你爸爸在等你呢
867. 我不知道她住在哪儿
868. 你觉得他怎么样
869. 现在我也喜欢
870. 我现在忙着呢
871. 你工作忙不忙
872. 请让我知道你想要什么
873. 我喜欢你的房间
874. 你累了对吧
875. 我们可以一起去
876. 他明天要去游泳吗
877. 我们已经准备好了
878. 您想再来点茶吗
879. 您从哪儿来的
880. 希望他明天会来吧
881. 对了你做什么工作的
882. 别在教室里说话
883. 我知道他的名字
884. 我爱我的妻子
885. 您在教室里吃了吗
886. 你为什么不做

887. 他说他太忙了
888. 这星期他会很忙
889. 都是猫的错
890. 您有手机吗
891. 我们不知道要做什么
892. 我明天去问他
893. 我还能做什么呢
894. 我给你介绍介绍我的朋友
895. 我还没有准备好
896. 我知道你会来的
897. 问他去火车站的路
898. 我有个问题
899. 我们现在非常忙
900. 我什么也没有告诉你
901. 我们可以玩儿也可以唱歌
902. 那家人还没起床
903. 我不知道你在看东西
904. 我也喜欢这个颜色
905. 你吃了多少鱼
906. 他问我买了些什么
907. 学生都笑了
908. 我们会很忙

909. 我知道的太多了
910. 别问我这是什么东西
911. 他不会高兴的
912. 你今天忙吗
913. 我正在听她唱歌
914. 你还等什么呢
915. 爸爸你喜欢面条吗
916. 在笑什么呢
917. 我让门开着
918. 你会游泳吗
919. 你能等一下吗
920. 我们喜欢一起唱歌
921. 你给了他什么
922. 什么问题都没有
923. 明天下午你忙吗
924. 她不喜欢米饭和面条
925. 你去玩儿好吗孩子
926. 电影什么时候开始
927. 哪本是您的书
928. 那你会给我什么
929. 我希望能再看见她
930. 这是谁的你知道吗
931. 她会是个好妻子的

932. 她问我怎么做鱼
933. 你今天晚上吃了什么
934. 准备明天的考试
935. 您想喝点什么吗
936. 你不听他的那就错了
937. 他什么都不知道
938. 你是说着玩儿的吧
939. 请穿点东西
940. 我觉得太大了
941. 我想买西瓜
942. 我吃得太多了
943. 这是我在报纸看的
944. 没有人会知道
945. 我们明天再来
946. 下午一起去游泳吧
947. 我有东西要给你
948. 为什么今天火车站没有出租车
949. 我非常喜欢中国菜
950. 你知道你在做什么吗
951. 每个人都知道他的名字
952. 别再给我打电话
953. 别再玩儿了
954. 明天我给你打电话

955. 别告诉他我在这儿
956. 我不喜欢吃面条
957. 如果你有什么不明白的就问吧
958. 我喜欢狗我妹妹喜欢猫
959. 我爸爸很忙
960. 现在让我们开始工作
961. 她问这怎么可能
962. 让我们去看电影好吗
963. 我很高兴和你在一起
964. 大家去工作吧
965. 我们一开始就知道
966. 我很累我想去睡觉
967. 你在忙什么
968. 我还可以来吗
969. 你的女儿很高
970. 她正在那儿打篮球
971. 是的我知道
972. 我希望你弟弟好点了
973. 他说我们休息一下
974. 你有问题吗
975. 你在笑什么呢
976. 我想你很忙
977. 我也很高兴认识你
978. 他爱学习也爱运动

979. 你最喜欢什么运动
980. 我能和老师说话吗
981. 大家在说什么呢
982. 你知道这是谁写的字吗
983. 不可能做得到
984. 他已经走了吗
985. 这给了我新的希望
986. 你为什么在跑步
987. 我也想知道
988. 你在找什么
989. 谁给你这个的
990. 没有人会再听了
991. 我们谁也不认识
992. 那你姐姐呢
993. 这是我的错
994. 你知道我在做什么吗
995. 大家都喜欢他
996. 你明天要踢足球
997. 明天天气可能很好
998. 你可以吃你喜欢的东西
999. 他都告诉我了
1000. 我知道你的名字
1001. 你最喜欢哪门课
1002. 大家都准备好了

1003. 你会跳舞吗

1004. 他不喜欢吃鱼

1005. 你什么都知道对吗

1006. 他不可能生病了

1007. 她的书卖得很好

1008. 我们是怎么知道的呢

1009. 我想知道她去哪儿了

1010. 他是什么时候开始踢足球的

1011. 我在晚上工作

1012. 我什么时候可以去看

1013. 你开得太快了

1014. 你能告诉我你为什么喜欢她吗

1015. 好吧你要走就走吧

1016. 她希望有个孩子

1017. 谢谢你打电话给我

1018. 现在您忙吗

1019. 她坐着唱歌

1020. 你为什么不在学校打篮球

1021. 我不知道要穿什么

1022. 我们在找他

1023. 这有什么错

1024. 好了我要走了

1025. 我的哥哥是老师

1026. 妈妈给我准备了好吃的东西

1027. 你要走多远

1028. 你告诉她的时候

1029. 你知道他是谁吗

1030. 去看医生吧

1031. 什么都别问我

1032. 我知道你在做什么

1033. 这让我很高兴

1034. 你要喝点什么吗

1035. 我知道她是谁

1036. 请给我一点儿水

1037. 请给我一些水

1038. 我昨天很忙

1039. 今天我们要跳舞了

1040. 你为什么打电话给我

1041. 我的房间非常小

1042. 那是我们的问题吗

1043. 您在找什么

1044. 这怎么可能呢

1045. 要工作的时候

1046. 他问了我妈妈

1047. 有什么不对吗

1048. 椅子离门很远

1049. 我们开始累了

1050. 他问我为什么在笑

1051. 你可以读你喜欢的书

1052. 电影什么时间开始

1053. 今天是我姐姐的生日

1054. 你明天要做什么

1055. 请告诉我你的问题

1056. 我知道你多大了

1057. 我很希望你会再来

1058. 他是我哥哥的朋友

1059. 我想和你一起去

1060. 猫在喝你的牛奶

1061. 我觉得他很高兴

1062. 她什么都不知道

1063. 我等着我妈妈

1064. 今天晚上吃什么

1065. 我不在就别开始

1066. 你要多少钱

1067. 问他一下他的名字

1068. 我也喜欢你

1069. 那孩子没有什么朋友

1070. 这是零的意思

1071. 他是来找工作的

1072. 你有弟弟吗

1073. 他给女儿买了新衣服

1074. 你喜欢坐哪儿就坐哪儿

1075. 我最喜欢吃面条

1076. 他要打篮球吗

1077. 我问他忙不忙

1078. 我非常喜欢我的工作

1079. 我不知道说什么

1080. 我想休息一下

1081. 我身体非常好

1082. 我一到了机场就打电话给你

1083. 电脑是新的

1084. 我不怎么看报纸

1085. 我们等来等去都看不见他

1086. 她买了报纸

1087. 你知道怎么说吗

1088. 你明天要来吗

1089. 她非常喜欢她的学校

1090. 等他来了我就走

1091. 我喜欢吃鱼和米饭

1092. 他已经穿好衣服了

1093. 这是你的房间吗

1094. 我已经买了它

1095. 都是我的错

1096. 我能知道你的名字吗

1097. 我很高兴你是对的

1098. 告诉我你想让我给你买什么

1099. 我好喜欢雪

1100. 你说得很对

1101. 你知道我的意思吗

1102. 要来点牛奶吗

1103. 我们什么时候到

1104. 我们可以去看电影吗

1105. 晚上可能会下雨

1106. 你让我快乐

1107. 他说离了题

1108. 我还可以再来吗

1109. 你能起床吗

1110. 我准备了羊肉

1111. 我们去打篮球吧

1112. 这是不可能的

1113. 我想去游泳

1114. 我可以看一下你的票吗

1115. 我的弟弟是老师

1116. 我昨天打电话给他

1117. 我很喜欢吃西瓜

1118. 我现在正在踢足球

1119. 我们要走多远

1120. 你为什么还在学校

1121. 你喜欢我就高兴

1122. 我和他一起走

1123. 我没有时间也没有钱

1124. 你要喝点茶吗

1125. 椅子离门很近

1126. 她很会唱歌

1127. 我喜欢你的咖啡

1128. 有件事情我要对你说

1129. 她开始唱歌了

1130. 出租车快来了

1131. 我不知道我们能做什么

1132. 我能给她打电话

1133. 她没走多远

1134. 宾馆有电脑吗

1135. 她可能会来

1136. 我不知道你在想什么

1137. 希望你会喜欢

Printed in Great Britain
by Amazon